THE

THE

Mobile MBA

112 SKILLS TO TAKE YOU FURTHER, FASTER

JO OWEN

Vice President, Publisher: Tim Moore
Associate Publisher and Director of Marketing: Amy Neidlinger
Acquisitions Editor: Megan Graue
Editorial Assistant: Pamela Boland
Operations Specialist: Jodi Kemper
Assistant Marketing Manager: Megan Graue
Cover Designer: Alan Clements
Managing Editor: Kristy Hart
Project Editor: Betsy Harris
Proofreader: Debbie Williams
Compositor: Glyph International
Manufacturing Buyer: Dan Uhrig

Published by Pearson Education, Inc.
Publishing as FT Press
Upper Saddle River, New Jersey 07458

Authorized adaptation from the original UK edition, entitled The Mobile MBA,
by Jo Owen, published by Pearson Education Limited, ©Jo Owen 2011.

This U.S. adaptation is published by Pearson Education, Inc.,

©2012 by arrangement with Pearson Education Ltd, United Kingdom.

FT Press offers excellent discounts on this book when ordered in quantity for bulk purchases or special
sales. For more information, please contact U.S. Corporate and Government Sales, 1-800-382-3419,
corpsales@pearsontechgroup.com. For sales outside the U.S., please contact International Sales at
international@pearsoned.com.

Printed in the United States of America

First Printing May 2012

ISBN-10: 0-13-306633-9
ISBN-13: 978-0-13-306633-3

Pearson Education LTD.
Pearson Education Australia PTY, Limited.
Pearson Education Singapore, Pte. Ltd.
Pearson Education Asia, Ltd.
Pearson Education Canada, Ltd.
Pearson Educación de Mexico, S.A. de C.V.
Pearson Education—Japan
Pearson Education Malaysia, Pte. Ltd.

Library of Congress Cataloging-in-Publication Data
Owen, Jo.
  The mobile MBA : 112 skills to take your further, faster / Jo Owen.
    p. cm.
  Includes bibliographical references and index.
  ISBN 978-0-13-306633-3 (pbk. : alk. paper) -- ISBN 0-13-306633-9
  1. Management. 2. Business. I. Title.

HD31.O8463 2012
658--dc23
                          2012009996

Brief contents

Contents

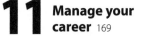

Introduction

An MBA is a curious beast: it can accelerate your career, even if it has limited practical value in day-to-day management.

Top employers hire top MBAs, but not because MBAs have mastered the mysteries of management. An MBA is a hallmark of personal commitment, effort, and ambition which employers value more than the actual content of the MBA course. Bayesian analysis, the Black Scholes option pricing model, and advanced corporate strategy are all more important in the MBA course than they are for a manager who is faced with a difficult customer, intransigent colleague, awkward boss, and a tight project deadline.

In practice, the MBA is a classic university course: it is very good at transferring a body of explicit knowledge from one generation to the next. Explicit knowledge is about "know-what" skills, like finance, accounting, math. This is useful knowledge to have. But as managers' careers progress, they find that technical skills become less important and people and political skills become more important. People and political skills are classic examples of tacit knowledge or "know-how." Universities and MBA courses are simply not very good at dealing with this sort of knowledge.

Like the MBA, the aim of this book is to help you accelerate your career, but not by simply reducing an MBA down to a few simplistic formulas. The aim is more ambitious than that.

This book assumes that you are smart. So *The Mobile MBA* does not spell out each MBA theory in detail: it is not trying to condense an entire MBA into one book. The purpose of *The Mobile MBA* is to show how you can apply MBA ideas in daily management practice. So the first part of the book breaks the key ideas of the MBA into bite-sized chunks and shows how you can use them.

If you already have an MBA you will discover how to use strategy, finance, accounting, marketing, organization, operations, math, and human capital *in practice*. If you don't have an MBA, this section will show you that there are no dark arts which only $60,000 and an MBA will reveal. It will demystify the mysteries of the MBA and lay out the simple principles which all managers must learn.

The second part of the book fills in the holes left by the MBA. It gives you a quick reference check to the survival skills of management. It is not a substitute for your personal experience: it is a sanity check for you. You can see if your experience is good or bad and if there are better ways of handling the endless ambiguous events which make management both challenging and rewarding.

You can read this book however you want. You do not have to start at the beginning and end at the end. You can dip in and out. You can keep it by your desk and use it as your just-in-time coach, to give you ideas and refresh your thinking when you face a tough challenge, or you can carry it with you, so you can use it on the way to meetings, workshops, or presentations. You can also use it alongside its online version. The address for this is **www.mobile-mba.com**. As well as this, the book comes with 11 free video *Skill-Pills*. These are brief training videos that can be downloaded to your smartphone, tablet, or computer. They will provide you with the skills and information needed to complete a task, wherever you are. Scan the QR code with your smartphone (you may have to download an app to help you do this). You can use the QR code that's inside the back cover of the book, or you can use the codes at the beginning of each chapter to take you straight to the interactive version. Keep that section on your phone or laptop and you will have the resource available to you wherever you go—you will have a truly mobile MBA in your hands.

Whether you have an MBA or not, *The Mobile MBA* is a very small investment in your future which can help you achieve very large returns. If *The Mobile MBA* helps you make the most of your career, it will have served its purpose.

1

The world of strategy

THE NATURE OF STRATEGY

The best predictor of next year's strategy is this year's strategy, plus or minus a bit. Most managers simply do not spend their lives re-inventing the firm's strategy every day. Even the CEO does not do this. Most strategy is incremental: it builds from one year to the next. Look at most of the top firms in the world and they have not radically changed their strategies for years.

dinosaurs can't dance

Firms that try to re-invent themselves as something different often fail: dinosaurs can't dance. Instead, most firms try to get better and better at what they already do, and then hope that no one else comes along with an idea which wipes out their business model.

Incremental strategy is risk averse: most businesses do not like risk, unless it is a guaranteed success. So the result is that most firms rise or fall with the market. In 1984 the FTSE 100 was created. It represented the very best of British business: the top 100 public companies. They appeared mighty and impregnable. By 2011, just 28 of them are still in the top 100. The problem is not that management has suddenly become incompetent. The problem is that the world has changed faster than they are able to change: strategic success formulas have become formulas for failure.

The reality of corporate strategy is far removed from the world of the gurus who teach strategy at business schools. But it pays to have an understanding of the two main schools of strategic thinking. Even to talk of "the two main schools of strategy" puts you far ahead of most of your peers. Here are the two schools:

The rationalists

The standard bearer for the rational school remains Michael Porter. His five forces analysis of industry claims that you can understand the attractiveness of an industry by assessing the strength of competitors, suppliers, customers, substitute products and services, and potential new market entrants. He leads a field which believes that analysis will provide the answer to most strategic challenges. Most top consulting firms believe that hard data and deep analysis are the way forward. Such a firm, BCG, invented the "BCG grid" which is a very analytical and prescriptive way of deciding how different businesses should be managed for cash, depending on their relative competitive position and the relative growth of their markets.

The rationalists face two practical challenges. The first is that messy, real-world reality often does not conform to crisp, clean models: how you choose to define a market can radically change the answers you get. The second practical problem is that if everyone does the same analysis and comes up with the same solution, you have a recipe for collective disaster. Success does not come from doing the same as all your competitors, but by being different in a relevant way. The good news for managers is that management has not yet been reduced to a few simple formulas: you still need smart management to deal with messy reality.

The romantics

There was a rebellion against the analytical types and their diagrams. The rebellion was led by C.K. Prahalad who showed that strategy is more a process of discovery than of analysis. You cannot predict the future, but you can discover it. Let us call this group the romantics, those who rebelled against the rationalists. Prahalad, supported by Gary Hamel, created two new ideas which have now found their way into mainstream management thinking: strategic intent and core competence. Prahalad was followed by other academics who he had trained including Chan Kim (blue ocean strategy) and Venkat Ramaswamy (co-creation).

Here is how their ideas stand apart from the rationalist tradition:

- **Strategic intent.** Instead of being constrained by analysis, strategic intent dares management to dream and plan for the seemingly impossible. The idea is to stretch the firm into business *not* as usual, to break the rules so that even smaller firms can challenge market leaders.

- **Core competence.** Instead of building points of differentiation around price, packaging, and performance which can be easily copied, build deep capabilities which cannot be copied quickly. Then exploit those capabilities across markets: for instance, Honda engine technology spreads from cars to outboard motors to motorbikes and mowers.

- **Blue ocean strategy.** Instead of competing in the red ocean of existing markets, where there is warfare for market share, discover uncharted new territories where you can succeed without competing: all the traditional analysis of markets and competitors disappears because you are competing in a completely new way.

- **Co-creation.** Instead of analyzing market needs and consumers, work with your users to identify what they most need. Let them help you develop and design new products and markets: treat them as partners, not just as customers.

Both have a place

In practice, both schools of strategy have their place in the sun. The rationalists tend to be better at incremental strategy for established and legacy organizations. The romantics tend to be better when you are looking for that radical break-through or you want to mobilize the organization for change. The rationalists separate developing and implementing strategy. For the romantics, developing and implementing strategy go hand in hand, and involve a much wider group of people, inside and beyond the firm, than the rationalists would normally involve.

DEALING WITH STRATEGY

If you want to succeed as a top manager, you have to show you can handle a strategic discussion.

An MBA course may let you believe that you can fix a company's strategy by reading case notes and analyzing sheets of data. But in reality it is not that simple. There is always ambiguity and uncertainty. But you need to know how to handle a strategic discussion in your organization. Instead of having smart answers, you need to have smart questions.

instead of having smart answers, you need to have smart questions

The process of strategy formulation is mainly about seeing things from a series of different perspectives, and asking the right questions about each perspective. Each perspective not only gives you a different view but may be in conflict with the others. There are no simple answers, so the discussion is important and you need to be able to contribute to it intelligently.

Here are the six main perspectives you need to think about and the typical sorts of question you need to be able to ask:

- **Customers.** What do they want? Are there under-served segments? Are there unfilled needs? How big and profitable is the potential of each market segment? Can we change our pricing or product for different customer segments (types)? How can we serve our existing customers better, retain them for longer, and make more money from each one? How can we acquire new customers more effectively and efficiently? What can we learn from our heavy users and from customers who defect? Can we grow into any new geographic markets?

- **Competitors.** Have they left any unserved segments or markets? Can we build any barriers to entry? Do we have any advantage (costs, brand, location, service) which the competitors cannot copy? What is their advantage over us? Do they have any profit sanctuaries we can disrupt? How will they react to any move we make? How fast and well can they copy us?

- **Channels.** What is our best route to market both for acquiring new customers and for serving new customers? What is the cost and effectiveness of each channel? Are there any new channels or partnerships to test and to build?

- **Product.** Can we use or adapt our product for another market or territory? Are there other offerings in other markets or from our competitors which we can learn from or improve? What is wrong with existing products? How easy or hard is it to copy our product and how can we defend it? Can we adapt or develop our existing products further and can we extend our brands any further? Are there any disruptive technologies out there which are either a threat or an opportunity for us?

- **Economics.** What is the cost to serve (and potential profitability) of each segment? Can we be lowest cost sustainably? How can we play with our cost structure (fixed and variable) and pricing structure to cause maximum damage to competitors? How can we use our suppliers and supply chain to better effect? Can we reduce our cost base through efficiency, re-engineering, outsourcing, partnerships? Should we look at game changing acquisitions: to fill out our product portfolio, to gain market access, or to reduce costs?

- **Corporate perspective.** This is where theory meets reality. You may be asked to dream the dream and be creative, but ultimately you will be rewarded not for taking a massive risk but for finding the incremental gain which drives the business forward: business is risk averse. Second, from a corporate perspective you will be rewarded for following the vision and agenda of the top team: your brilliant idea will remain a pipe dream if it does not fit with the corporate agenda.

Keep pushing at different perspectives and you will eventually find a new insight. Chase the insight, not consensus. Consensus will lead to a me-too strategy where you follow competition. Insight will drive you to a new place altogether.

APPLYING STRATEGY TO YOUR AREA

If you want to make a difference and be visible to top management, align what you do with top management's strategy. This is known as a BFO: a blinding flash of the obvious. It is so obvious that it is routinely missed by most managers. Many departments simply keep on pushing the agenda they inherited, instead of thinking what is really needed. Just as the best predictor of next year's strategy is this year's strategy, so the best predictor of next year's departmental budget is this year's budget. The incremental approach is low risk at both corporate and departmental level. But at some point, incremental paths slowly diverge. You need to bring them back together again, and be seen to be doing so.

Even if the overall corporate strategy changes little, the language and emphasis will change from year to year and from CEO to CEO. The focus will shift from customers to products to costs to quality to globalization and back to customers again. Essentially, the CEO and top management are telling a story about what they think is important, and one they want you to follow. This is your chance to shine: show that you understand the new focus and that you are doing something about it. You will immediately set yourself apart from your peers who are doing business as usual.

The question is: how do you show you are being strategy driven? A simple and real case will make the point (see below).

If the facilities manager can act strategically, anyone can.

So what if you cannot effect a strategic revolution to align your area with the corporate strategy? The next best thing is to make sure you talk the language of the new priorities. So if the new priority is about customer focus, highlight all the work that you do that is customer focused and show how you are increasing that focus in your unit. Talking this way will be music to the ears of top managers who are normally very frustrated that their ideas are neither fully understood nor fully implemented throughout the organization: you will sound different and stand out from your peers for all the right reasons.

A simple case

You are the facilities manager for a professional services firm. The new CEO has decided that the firm needs to be more client focused and more collaborative. So what on earth does that have to do with you? You generally worry about non-client focused things like coffee machines, office cleaning, and where the desks should be placed.

But you are different. You realize that this is your chance to make a difference and to shine. So you start by changing the layout of the office. To encourage staff to spend time with clients, you introduce hot desking with not enough desks to go around for all the staff. To encourage a more collaborative workplace, you replace executives' private offices with an open plan space. You then work with IT to replace all the desktops with laptops so that executives can travel and spend more time with clients. In essence, you effect a strategic revolution.

FOUR PILLARS OF STRATEGY

Most business strategies are very simple. They all pass the elevator test: "Can you explain your strategy to an investor on a short ride in an elevator?" Executing the strategy is harder than describing it. Most strategies are built on one of four basic pillars: customers, products, competition, or economics. Each pillar gives a different insight and different approach:

- **Customer led.** Solve a customer problem or need; build a brand and franchise. FMCG (fast moving consumer goods) are the natural home of customer focused businesses. New entrants will often solve an existing or unknown customer need in a unique way. The successful dot.com businesses delivered a customer need, like Facebook and Amazon. The dot.com failures fell in love with the product and technology (Boo.com, Webvan) and failed.

- **Product led.** Build a better mousetrap; build a new product development machine. Pharmaceutical companies are classic product innovation machines. But old markets can be upset by new entrants coming in with new products to disrupt the incumbents: think of Dyson in vacuum cleaners and Amazon in book retailing. It was very hard for the incumbents to follow.

- **Competitively focused.** Can we stay level with or beat our peers? Incumbents tend to be in oligopolies where they follow each other with minor differences. New entrants come in with completely new approaches: think of the major airlines and the rapid arrival and growth of the low-cost carriers.

- **Economically focused.** Achieve economies of scale; lowest cost producer. Oil and gas firms are obvious examples. Many large car firms became obsessed with cost and economies of scale and forgot their customer focus and product quality, leaving the way open for new entrants from Japan.

To make it more complicated, there are differences between new entrants into the market and incumbents. Typically, incumbents layer one advantage on top of another. New entrants seek a big advantage in one area: they practice asymmetric warfare. Successful new entrants change the rules of the game in ways which the incumbents cannot follow. Here are some simple examples to make the point:

Strategy type	Incumbents	New entrants
Customer focused	P&G, Unilever, Coca-Cola	Virgin, Facebook
Product focused	Pharmaceutical firms	Dyson, Skype
Competitively focused	Major airlines, banks	Ryanair
Economically focused	Oil and gas majors, miners	Dell as a start up, Formule 1

New entrants succeed not by copying the incumbents, but by being different. But their formula can be copied by other new entrants, so they quickly have to raise their game and start layering in new advantages. So Microsoft started out as product focused (by providing an operating system for early IBM PCs) and then became competitively focused, now dominating the market for desktop operating systems. Google followed suit. It started as product focused by providing a fast search facility, then built a unique economic model of paid search and finally is becoming competitively focused as it seeks to dominate the global market for organizing the world's information. Google's original product advantage was easy to copy; the economic model of paid search was harder to follow because Google had scale and reach others could not match. The final, competitive advantage of organizing the world's information is so scale-sensitive it will be very hard for anyone to follow.

If you are an incumbent, strategy will be incremental and low risk: expand a product range or channel, reassess investment priorities. If you are a new entrant, do not play the incumbent's game. Change the rules of the game so that the incumbents cannot follow you, and then change the rules of the game again so that other new entrants cannot follow you.

STRATEGY AND THE ART OF UNFAIR COMPETITION

The goal of strategy is very simple: you have to find a source of unfair competition which results in making excess profits. Regulators and competitors should hate you for this, but without it, you fail. Every firm needs to make "excess" profits somewhere to stay alive: this profit sanctuary will help to pay for all the projects that go wrong, for investments that take time to mature, and to offset the impact of competition, customers, taxpayers, and staff who always seem to want more and give less.

You can only make excess profits if you have a source of unfair competition somewhere. All successful businesses have some form of unfair advantage, which other competitors find very hard to copy. For instance, you may:

- Have a license to drill oil in a low cost oil field (e.g. Exxon, Petrobas, Shell)

- Be in the best location on Main Street (e.g. McDonald's, Starbucks)

- Own copyright or patents (e.g. Disney, Dyson, hi-tech firms)

- Be the first to move into a new market and dominate it (e.g. Google and paid search, Microsoft and desktop operating systems)

- Have a powerful brand (e.g. P&G, Unilever, Nike)

- Have a global network which is hard to copy (e.g. McKinsey and Goldman Sachs)

- Own a unique resource (e.g. Heathrow landing slots)

If you and your firm talk about "points of differentiation," be very worried. That is a weak form of competitive advantage. Your goal is to have a thoroughly unfair advantage which allows you to make large amounts of money. The problem with a fair fight is that you might lose it: make sure the competitive fight is as unfair as possible.

What is your source of unfair competitive advantage?

PORTFOLIO STRATEGY

Portfolio strategy is a classic MBA lesson. But as with some theories, the realities can be a stranger to the practice when it comes to corporate level strategy. The two main issues are that portfolio strategy is a flawed theory and practicing leaders think of their portfolio in a different way.

Outline of the theory

Your investment strategy is determined by the relative competitive position of your business and by the growth rate of its market. This gives rise to the following prescriptions:

- High relative competitive position, high growth market: reinvest cash to maintain share

- High relative competitive position, low growth market: milk the product for cash

- Low relative competitive position, high growth market: sell the business

- Low relative competitive position, low market growth: exit, close, sell

The theory breaks down as soon as it hits reality. The first big problem is about defining your market and your relative competitive position. For instance, Flash was a powdered floor cleaner with 45% share of a declining market (the powdered market). But if it was seen as part of all floor cleaners (including liquids and creams) it had about 20% of a growing market. Depending on the definition, you could say it was growing or declining and be perceived as a market leader or a me-too brand. How you define the brand defines your strategy.

The second problem with this approach is that if everyone follows it, you have collective marketplace insanity. For instance, milling and baking is a dull and declining business in many mature markets. So you would want to run it for cash or exit it. The more you run the business down, the more portfolio theory becomes a self-fulfilling prophecy. As no one invests in it, the industry disappears as surely as the Cheshire Cat leaving nothing but a smile behind. The same thinking would apply to steel and other mature industries.

Practicing leaders think of portfolio strategy differently

If you are in an industry then that is your business and your future. It does not matter whether the theory says it should be growing or declining. As a leader, your job is to make the most of your business. So you should protect and grow it. If you are a steel maker, you could argue that making computer games is a more attractive industry with more growth and better margins. But that does not mean you should ditch steel and enter computer games. Your investors can make that decision in order to protect their investment portfolios, but you have your business to run. And even if the whole industry is in decline, there is still plenty of room for you to succeed:

- In the steel industry, Nucor grew by adopting a radically different model from the incumbents (recycling, mini mills versus large integrated mills).

- In milling and baking, RHM saw that other players were running their operations down. So they invested in their own milling and baking operations to make them the best and at lowest cost; they built share and protected margins.

Let shareholders worry about their portfolios; they can diversify at very low cost. As a leader, focus on your mission rather than worry about portfolio balance.

THE WORLD OF STRATEGY

CREATING A VISION FOR YOUR FIRM AND YOUR TEAM

A vision is a story in three parts:

- This is where we are.

- This is where we are going.

- This is how we will get there.

And if you want to make the vision truly compelling, you add a fourth part: "and here is your very important role in helping us get there." In other words, make the vision personal. Telling people that your vision is to increase earnings per share by 7% for the next five years is not wildly exciting: instead show how achieving this will help create growth and more job opportunities for all.

Often the best visions are the simplest: "We will become more customer focused," "We are going to become international," "We will professionalize our operations." These are simple statements that everyone can understand, and they give you a script to follow for the rest of the year. If you are running a large organization, you may want a grander vision.

often the best visions are the simplest

If you want a big vision, try this one: "We will put a man on the moon within ten years." Kennedy's vision, in the wake of Sputnik, seemed like a pipe dream. But it was achieved. Since the vision, NASA has had successes and failures (Hubble and Challenger), but has lost its way compared to the time it was driven by Kennedy's compelling vision.

To test your firm's vision, think of Kennedy, NASA, the space race and Russia. RUSSIA is the acronym for what makes a good vision:

- **R**elevant: it meets a need which everyone inside the firm can recognize.

- **U**nique: you could not apply your vision to your competitors or to the local coffee shop.

- **S**tretching: "I will go to work most days" is not a great vision. "I will conquer the known world by the age of 30" is a bit more stretching: step forward Alexander the Great.

- **S**imple: if no one can remember it, no one can act on it.

- **I**mmediate: you have to act on the vision now and know when you have gotten there.

- **A**ctionable: each person in the firm must know what it means for them, and the firm must know how the vision will affect investment, decision making, measurements, and rewards.

How Russian is the vision for your firm and your team?

MERGERS AND ACQUISITIONS

For the past 30 years at least, academic studies have shown that most acquisitions destroy value for the shareholders of the acquiring firm. The only winners are the shareholders of the acquired firm who typically enjoy a 40% bid premium on the shares they sell.

For CEOs, M&A activity is very attractive: it shows that you are doing something dramatic, it allows you to tell a story and it is quicker and easier than the grind of building the business organically. It also gives you a larger empire to run. For investment banks, M&A activity means fees for the acquirer and for the defense; fees for negotiating the funding; fees for then breaking up the merger and sorting out the financial mess five years later.

There are essentially three sorts of acquisition:

- The unrelated acquisition where the financial plays succeed in the medium term but few survive long term: the acquired company has little or nothing in common with the holding company. The acquirers used to be conglomerates like ITT or Hanson; nowadays they are likely to be private equity firms. In each case, the message is that the acquirer has found a superior way of managing any sort of firm. In practice, it relies on financial engineering (conglomerates) and large amounts of leverage (private equity). When times are good, profits rise and the acquirers look like geniuses. When recession hits and profits fall, they discover the dark side of leverage, which can be very dark indeed.

- The fill-in acquisition where the acquisitions become very expensive: this is designed to fill in a hole in a firm's technology, capability, or market coverage. IBM has been buying dozens of mid-scale firms for precisely this reason: building a portfolio of competences fast. Arguably, it is cheaper to buy a market tested competence than try to build it internally. However, since every other major technology player has had the same idea, you will pay a high premium for your acquisitions.

- The scale acquisition, in industries where you face a simple choice: you can be predator or prey. "Economies of scale" are the holy grail of many acquisitions. The scale acquisition works in two ways. Internally, it enables the firm to reduce unit costs: you reduce staffing levels, and reduce infrastructure spend on IT, facilities, factories, and the supply chain. Externally, it enables the firm to increase market dominance over both suppliers (by forcing them to reduce prices) and customers (removing market capacity and competition enables prices to rise). Inevitably, regulators become very interested when the scale acquisition leads to excess market dominance. Retailing banking for the past 30 years has been swamped by scale driven M&As, with huge savings to be made in people, property, and IT.

The fatal flaw with most acquisitions is that the acquirer pays too much for the acquisition. The logic of the deal may be right, but the price is often wrong. This happens because the thrill of the hunt overwhelms any logic. Investment bankers will be whispering in your ear, "Dare to be great." The media will portray it as a hunt: you either get your kill or you have failed as a CEO.

The only known antidote to the madness of the hunt is a used envelope. On the back of it, work out the maximum you are prepared to pay for the target, with all the economies of scale. Do this before the hunt starts. Then keep the envelope in your pocket. If you are invited to pay too much, refer to your envelope and walk away. Ignore all the clever arguments of advisers who will always find ways of justifying an ever higher price: a used envelope has more integrity and impartiality than your highly paid advisers. And it costs less.

HOW TO BE INNOVATIVE

All firms and clients say they like innovation. They lie. They like the results of successful innovation, which may lead to a source of unfair competitive advantage. But they hate the process of innovation. Next time you are asked to innovate, ask in return if your managers enjoy risk, ambiguity, uncertainty, expense, and failure. Then you will find out how much firms really want innovation. Innovation is fine as long as it is tried, tested and bound to succeed.

Fortunately, you do not have to discover the successor to the wheel to innovate. Nor do you have to endure sessions with your "creatives." Here is how you can find an innovative idea:

1 **Copy an idea, especially from abroad.** The low-cost carrier model was developed by SouthWest Airlines in the USA and its success was obvious. It took 10 years before Ryanair and easyJet copied the model into Europe with devastating results.

2 **Find a solution for a customer problem.**

3 Listen to your customers. The useful ones are either the heavy users, or the awkward squad who are always complaining. They are the ones who will have the ideas and insights about what the market really needs. See if you can deliver it profitably.

4 Spend a day in the life of your customer. See what they world looks like from their end as they try to use your product or service. It can be a humbling experience, but profitable. Take it further and co-create the new service with your client.

5 Find a market failure and do something about it. As a middle market company, I found banks overcharging me on prices, being inefficient, and selling awful products. That was great news: I set up a bank which was slightly less bad and it took off. Don't get mad, get even.

Finding the idea is perhaps 10% of the battle. The real battle is internal: making sure that you have the support and commitment of the organization to make the idea happen.

THE LANGUAGE OF STRATEGY

Some managers love to throw around strategic words to make themselves and their ideas sound impressive. In practice, when a manager says something is "strategic" they mean it is important, but perhaps only to themselves. Here are some of the most common concepts, what they mean and how you can use them.

STRATEGIC INTENT Normally used as a way of making a goal sound impressive. As used in practice by the late C.K. Prahalad (who came up with the term) it was a way of stretching the organization and daring managers to achieve things which would force business *not* as usual. The intellectual integrity of the idea is weak, but the stories used to illustrate the idea are inspirational.

CORE COMPETENCE This is generally used to refer to anything we think we might be good at doing. This also came from C.K. Prahalad, and is more inspirational than practical.

CO-CREATION This is a Venkat Ramaswamy concept and gets very complicated very fast. At its simplest, it means we want to work with our customers a bit more, especially by involving them in product development. Many great ideas come from users, so it makes sense to listen to them and work with them.

It is much more than "giving customers control," which is a euphemism for cutting out your help desk and giving your customers a web link instead.

BLUE OCEAN, RED OCEAN Brought to us courtesy of Chan Kim. The basic arguments are simple: try to compete in uncompeted territory (easier for start-ups than for legacy businesses). Second, draw a value curve of what customers really want, and then re-engineer your product to focus on that and nothing else. This often leads to the birdie strategy (birds go cheep cheep and this strategy often leads to going cheap cheap).

REENGINEERING More of an operational play than a true strategy. Originally it meant working out what the customer really wanted and then reorganizing the processes of the organization to deliver that well. It was a revolution because it made people look at a horizontal view of the organization (processes) not the old vertical view (functional silos). It has now become a short-hand for cost cutting which ignores the customer completely.

VALUE PROPOSITION At its simplest, this means giving customers what they want at a price they want. This leads to value curves: map the value customers want versus what you give and what competitors give. Analyze the value curve to do some value engineering: cut out what customers do not want and reduce your costs, while focusing on what customers most want.

PORTFOLIO STRATEGY AND MANAGEMENT Work out which businesses or products you want to exit, stay in, build, and grow. Ultimately, the portfolio strategy should enable the firm to achieve a balance of cash producing and cash consuming (but growing) businesses. In practice, very few managers ever do a portfolio strategy and when they do, they get bogged down in definitions of the market, relative growth, and relative share.

your competitive advantage should be thoroughly unfair

COMPETITIVE ADVANTAGE, DIFFERENTIATION Listen carefully when people talk about this. Often they refer to very weak advantages ("we are a penny cheaper; our packaging is nicer..."). These are weak advantages because they are easy to copy. To be relevant, your competitive advantage should be thoroughly unfair, that means it has to be:

- **Sustainable**: price cuts are often not sustainable.

- **Hard to copy**: copying a financial product takes minutes; copying a patent or a copyright leads straight to court. Copying Microsoft's near monopoly on desktop operating systems is not easy.

GO TO MARKET STRATEGY This means more or less what people want it to mean. It can refer to your firm's:

- **Overall strategy**: how will we deploy our assets and capabilities to achieve our goals?

- **Marketing strategy**: which customers will we target, through which channels, at what price, and how will we position our product relative to competition?

- **Channel strategy**: we know our product and our target customer, but how will we reach them in terms of sales, advertising, and the route to market (which channels of distribution will we use)?

BUSINESS START-UPS

You need to decide if running a business is for you. Here is what to expect.

Before you start, people will tell you it won't work. When you start, they will tell you it isn't a real business. Finally, when you are in your private jet and they are negotiating their 10% pay raise, they will tell you that you were lucky and that they were absolutely central to your success. As you build the business you will find about 50 people who believe that they each deserve 10% of the equity for their help, for their advice, and for the introductions they made for you. And then they wonder why entrepreneurs can be arrogant.

Moving from salaried security to insecure start-up is a one-way leap: you can never go back. Once you have tasted the joys and hell of freedom you cannot return to the gilded cage of employment. You may work longer and for less money, but psychologically you will find it impossible to work for someone else. At least on your own, your triumphs and disasters are all your own.

The leap is huge. You are not just changing employment: you are changing your identity. You no longer get the kudos from saying, "I am the big chief at MegaCorp." You are your business: failure is not just a business failure, it is failure of your dreams and identity. This is hard in a way that business school can never prepare you for. You discover that if your computer goes down, it is a disaster and no one is there to save the day for you. Cash flow is not a few lines on the monthly report: it is the difference between paying the bills and going bankrupt. Weekends and holidays are a luxury that salaried colleagues enjoy and you do not. But, if this is what you want, then go for it. The ride is exciting, exhilarating, and exhausting. And you will never turn back.

Second, you need to know how to go about it. Again, business schools are too sophisticated in their approach. In practice, I have followed a simple model with each business I have started: IPM. IPM stands for ideas, people, money. You need them in that order: ideas first, then people, and finally money. It tends to go wrong when people start with the money ("I want $10 million in five years") and work back from that. Everyone starts to argue over a pot of money which does not exist, instead of building the business. Here is IPM in more detail:

I: IDEA You need a great idea which you believe in 100%. It can be as simple as "there is no hairstylist in this town (and I like styling hair)" through to the most ambitious of global start-ups. Be very clear about why your idea will:

● Attract and retain many customers

● Be sustainably competitive

● Make money: the economics should be robust

Don't be afraid to discuss your "secret" idea with other people. In practice, no one else is likely to have the energy and motivation to take the leap you propose, and they will not understand the full scope of your idea anyway. As you discuss the idea, they will raise many objections. Good ideas simply get stronger as a result of overcoming each objection. As you share your idea, you will also find some people who could be very good partners for you. You are doing soft recruiting for your new venture.

Be ambitious with your idea. The more ambitious it is, the more likely you are to attract great talent. Which leads to the well worn motto: "Think big, start small, scale fast." When you start, you may start as a small business, but be clear about how you will realize its full potential and become a big business.

At this stage, it makes sense to develop your idea from the safety of your current employer. Regular income is a wonderful thing to have.

P: PEOPLE A sole trader business is a lifestyle business. It is often hard to sustain for long. To succeed, you need to have a great team around you. Pick people who complement your skills: they should be different from you in terms of both skills and styles. Not everyone wants to do accounting, or sales, or IT: find those skills. And if you only hire extroverts, your office will have all the order of a chimpanzees' tea party. If you hire only introverts, your office will be like a library echoing to the sound of silence.

Recognize that you will probably have to turn your team over as the business grows. People who enjoy start-ups enjoy the buzz, freedom, and creativity that goes with them. These are not people who like the order, structure, systems, and discipline of a larger organization.

M: MONEY A good idea beats the dull weight of money every time. And if you have a great idea and great people, you will find the money. If you lack the idea or the people, then you will never get the money. The idea and the people always have to come first.

a good idea beats the dull weight of money every time

Fortunately, there are many sources of funding for you to tap: venture capitalists, banks, exorbitant credit cards, your own piggy bank, angel investors (who can turn into devils), unsuspecting relatives, and of course customers and suppliers if you manage your cash flow properly. If you have great people, you will work the money out. And you will probably have a few financial near-death experiences along the way. In years to come, they will be the war stories you fondly remember.

Finally, remember that equity is everything. Everyone will want a slice of your action. Don't give it. It's your business, so keep it that way.

2

Marketing and sales

INTRODUCTION

Marketing and sales follow naturally from strategy because most good strategies are based on a deep understanding of the market and the customer.

Marketing and sales people tend to be protective of their territory. Sales people rightly have pride in being the people that bring in all the money, and do not have much respect for those who do not. If you have been in a selling role yourself, you will be an honorary member of the club; otherwise do not try to get clever with the sales force and do not try telling them how they can improve their performance.

Marketing has evolved greatly over the years, and marketers have a habit of trying to bamboozle other executives with sophisticated sounding ideas. But despite all the changes, the fundamental principles of marketing have stayed the same and are remarkably simple. Genius does not come from making things complicated, it comes from making things simple. So if you can focus on the few simple principles below, you will not go too far wrong in marketing.

THE NATURE OF MARKETING

At business school they teach the four Ps and three Cs of marketing. The four Ps were developed by Philip Kotler:

- **Product**: what will we sell and what benefit will it offer?
- **Price**: how much will we sell it for?
- **Promotion**: how will we advertise to customers and promote our product?
- **Place**: what channels will we use to go to market?

Non-marketers observe that there is one P missing: profit. Marketing should be about making profits, not just about gaining market share and growing sales. The alternative version of this is the three Cs, which Kotler also developed:

- **Customers**: what sort of customers (segments) will we target?
- **Competitors**: who are our rivals and how are we different and better than them in a way that is sustainable and hard for them to copy?
- **Channels**: how will we reach our customers in terms of sales, marketing, and distribution?

Again, the non-marketers observe that there is a missing C: costs. Marketing can be a very expensive discipline and managing costs is hard, because you cannot immediately relate marketing costs to either sales or production. It is an investment which pays off in the longer term. The four Ps and three Cs ignore profits (the fifth P) and costs (the fourth C), which is why marketers used to have a bad name. Today, marketers ignore profits and costs at their peril.

most effective strategy starts with the logic of the marketplace

A marketing driven firm will understand the needs of the market and will drive the logic of the market back through all that the firm does. Most effective strategy starts with the logic of the marketplace. In contrast, many firms become very internally focused and lose sight of the market. Classically, Ford succeeded in the early days by creating the world's first moving production line. It was supplanted by GM who took a more customer focused view of the world. Ford promised customers could have a car in any color, as long as it was black. GM promised a car for "every purse and purpose": the world of market segmentation and customer focus had arrived.

THE ADVERTISING BRIEF

Dealing with advertising agencies is to enter a parallel universe where people will say things like "wonderful production values; sans serif is much more authoritative; this curve is very dynamic." They will be deeply offended if you start laughing at such nonsense: they genuinely think that they are being deeply insightful. You are meant to be impressed, overawed, and feel privileged to pay their fees. There is only one known antidote to such talk: a good advertising brief. A good advertising brief has four parts:

- **Target audience:** to whom are we trying to communicate? "Everyone" is a bad answer. Targeting multiple groups is also unhelpful, because they will probably want different things. Make your target audience as focused as possible. You should be able to imagine your target buyer as an individual.

- **Benefits:** what is the distinctive benefit which we offer to our customer? Is it relevant to their needs and is it distinctive versus the competition? If the answer is more than 12 words long, it is too long.

- **Reason why:** why should our customer believe that we can deliver the benefit they want? What is it about our product or service that means it can do what we say it can do? Again, 12 words or less.

- **Brand character:** once more in 12 words or less. People do not just buy a benefit, they buy an image. In some cases, such as cosmetics, that is more or less all they buy. So what is the image of your brand and how will that appeal to your target customer?

Once you have a clear advertising brief, you have the basis for a sensible discussion about advertising. Instead of it being entirely subjective ("mauve is the must have color this year..."), you can have a semi-objective discussion about how far the advertising meets the brief. To be a true advertising expert, you then apply a few more criteria to the advertising you see, and that is the subject of the next section.

Typically, an advertising brief will need to be supported by a media strategy. The media strategy looks at which sort of media we will use (TV, Internet, posters, magazines, etc.) and then at how much coverage we want to achieve. This will normally be expressed as the amount of times our target audience will see our advertising in a specified period of time. If you have defined your target audience well, then the media strategy will follow naturally. If you are targeting multi-millionaires then advertising on daytime TV is probably not the most efficient way of reaching them.

HOW TO BE AN ADVERTISING EXPERT

P&G is one of the world's great marketing and advertising companies. Most of its advertising is controlled by brand managers who have recently graduated from a university or MBA school. So how do they create advertising experts out of such relatively inexperienced people? In practice, there are a few simple disciplines which they hammer home time and again, and which I learned marketing Daz, a detergent.

The first thing you discover is that you do not judge advertising by whether you like it or not. The purpose of advertising is not to entertain, it is to sell product, in my case Daz. Winning awards is irrelevant. It does not matter if people like the advertising: not everyone likes Daz advertising, but they remember it and they buy it. So the ultimate tests of any advertising are:

- Do people remember it?

- Do they buy the product?

To figure out if advertising is likely to work, before spending vast amounts of money, there are 10 tests you can apply. Apply this set to any advertising you see: you will find many campaigns are expensive failures, while others work even if you do not like them.

The 10 tests

1   Does it meet the brief we agreed? Daz washes whiter – OK?

2   Is it differentiated versus the nearest alternatives? Ariel for stains, Dreft for woollens: you get the idea.

3   Does it give a compelling reason why I should buy? If you do not want white clothes to look grey, buy Daz.

4   Is it relevant to the people we are targeting? For people with white clothes, yes.

5   Is it credible? Daz has the "blue whitener" to keep white clothes white. Give a reason why your product works.

6   Is the brand clear? Forget celebrities and clever artistry: stick the brand up front so people remember Daz, not the artistry or celebrity.

7   Does it project the character of the brand? Daz is cheap and cheery, versus high tech Ariel, etc.

8   Is it simple and memorable? One brand, one message: Daz washes whiter.

9   Is it consistent with other material? Easy to use on TV, radio, posters, magazines.

10 Is it sustainable economically and creatively over time? Daz advertising has not changed in 50 years, because it works.

THE MARKETING BRIEF

You do not need to be a marketing expert to contribute to the marketing discussion. Often, marketing is not about knowing all the answers, but about
asking smart questions. The best questions are the simplest ones, which cut to
the heart of the business. And the best way of getting to the heart of the business is to focus on the marketing strategy.

At the heart of a marketing strategy is the advertising strategy and we've just
covered this:

● Target audience
● Product benefit

- Reason why
- Brand character

Clearly, there is more to marketing than advertising. So the full marketing strategy needs a few more elements. Here they are:

- **Media strategy:** how are we going to communicate with our target audience? How often will we communicate with them and through what media?
- **Pricing strategy:** how will we price our product? You have several choices:
  - Cost plus: add a fixed margin to our costs. But this takes no account of what customers want to pay and how much competitors charge.
  - Price to value: work out the value that the customer gets, and price to that.
  - Price relative to competition: "We will charge a 10% premium/discount versus our main competitor."
- **Channel strategy:** how will we sell to our target audience? What channels will we use?
- **Product strategy:** how will we develop our product so that it stays relevant to customers and remain competitive in the marketplace? How will we present and package our product in line with the advertising brief?

marketing strategy is a process of asking very simple questions, which are very hard to answer

The best marketing strategies have a clear strategy for test markets and market research. Creating a marketing strategy is a process of asking very simple questions, which are very hard to answer with any confidence. Test marketing and market research are the best ways to find out many of the answers, and to ensure that you keep your offering relevant and competitive in the marketplace.

If you want a productive discussion with your marketing colleagues, do not focus on whether you like the packaging, advertising, or product smell. It is a subjective discussion which leads nowhere. Focus instead on the marketing strategy and goals. If the strategy is clearly being followed, then do not waste time arguing over the detail: trust the professionals to execute it properly.

MARKET SEGMENTATION

Not all customers are the same. They differ in size, profitability, and cost to serve. They have different needs. Each different type of customer is potentially a different market segment. Many great strategies are based on this simple insight. You can find market segmentation all around you:

● The car market is segmented by price, need, and lifestyle. Ferraris, Minis, and off-road vehicles all represent different markets and different customer segments.

● Your bank will treat you differently depending on the value of your account: with services going all the way from standard retail offerings, to high end private banking where a relationship manager will actually know you and your family personally.

● Washing powders are classics of market segmentation with different products for stains (Ariel), delicate fabrics (Dreft), softening and cleaning (Bold), white clothes (Daz) and all-round family cleaning (Persil), alongside cheaper own label brands.

Market segmentation is also essential in the business-to-business market. Consulting firms and banks segment their clients by size and industry, so they can offer specialist services to each type of industry customer. Chemical companies can specialize by size of customer: larger customers get more specialized support and products than smaller customers. Paint companies segment by customer need: car manufacturers, house builders, aerospace, and domestic customers all have very different needs and pricing.

What a market segment looks like

How do you test to ensure you have a viable market segment? It must be:

● **Unique:** a customer cannot belong to two segments at the same time.

● **Actionable:** you must be able to identify who belongs to each segment and treat them differently. Serving different age groups or regions is fairly simple. Identifying and serving people who are whimsical, arrogant, or playful is much harder and is probably not actionable.

● **Sustainable and durable:** if you want to go to the expense of serving a group of customers in a unique way, you need the group to be big enough to be worth serving.

Serving different market segments

In practice, you have a market segment when you treat one group of customers differently from another. In the jargon of the day, you serve each segment with a different value proposition, which means you will:

- Offer a different product or service variation to each different segment ("product differentiation")

- Maintain different prices for different customer groups ("price differentiation")

- Go to market in different ways: you may use different advertising channels and messages for each group

- Compete against different competitors in each segment

Market segmentation in practice

Unless you are responsible for marketing or strategy, you are unlikely to have to do a market segmentation exercise yourself. But segmentation should still inform your thinking on a range of topics.

Management discussions of "the market" or "the customer" are often very misleading because there is no average customer. You can offer insight to your colleagues by exploring different sorts of customer and need, and seeing how you can serve each segment best.

Reviewing market research could lead to a discussion of averages, which is at best useless and at worst dangerous. Provide insight by probing for the responses from different groups. If the average response is to rate a product 5/10, that may hide the "Marmite effect": some people love it (10/10) and some people hate it (0/10). This leads to a radically different action from focusing on the average response.

Profitability discussions often look at simple decisions such as "raising prices" or "lowering costs." Look at different market segments to find where you can best raise prices or lower costs without hurting the business.

HOW TO PRICE

Have you ever heard a customer or a sales person say that your prices are too low? The road to profit is higher prices. But all the pressure is to lower prices. So how do you price? There are three basic methods:

● **Cost plus:** add a margin to your basic (variable) costs and hope to make enough to cover your fixed costs and leave a profit. Very often this leads to underpricing, and low to no profit. A variation of cost plus is return on capital: this is used by regulators of utilities, normally with catastrophic effect.

the road to profit is higher prices

● **Price to competition:** typically this is called "follow the leader." Follow the market leader's pricing and add a premium or a discount according to where your product stands. The problem with this is that the market leader always wins: they have more volume and will make more money than you do on your lower volumes.

● **Price to value:** the customer has no interest in how much it costs you to produce your product or service. If you offer $100 of value and it costs you only $1 to deliver it, then the customer will still be happy if you charge $50 or even more. Your major constraint is competition.

How to raise the achieved price

Most organizations have a natural tendency to underprice: this shows a lack of confidence in the value that the firm offers in the marketplace, and has to be challenged. In practice, you have a range of options for raising the achieved price:

● **The pricing ladder.** The basic price is low, but the extras add up. So your flight costs $5, but then there is the booking charge, the seat reservation charge, the luggage charge, the check-in charge, the inflight services charges, taxes and suddenly you have been charged a fortune for your "bargain" flight. You can see pricing ladders at work in the selling of PCs and cars, which always seem to come with costly but attractive extras.

● **The price anchor.** Set a very high nominal price, then discount heavily against it. This is how wine and furniture are always being sold at 40% or 50% discounts. The retailer establishes a high price expecting no sales at that level, then they offer a "bargain sale" where they sell their products at a good margin.

● **The bait and switch.** Offer a low introductory price and once the customer is hooked, revert to "normal" pricing. You see this in phone packages, but also in business-to-business where consultants and contractors may offer to do the specifications and initial work cheaply or even for free: by the time they have finished you are hooked and cannot escape.

- **The price jumble.** This is a variation on the pricing ladder. Make your pricing so complicated that anyone trying to compare packages loses the will to live: think of mobile phone deals. There will always be some element of the jumble you can highlight as being top value.

- **The unique package.** The more standardized your market becomes, the harder it is to raise prices. So seek differentiation. Change the size of your packaging; change the form of your product; change the service and terms. Be different, create multiple price points and choice.

How not to price

- **Listen to sales person:** they always want a lower price.

- **Listen to customers:** they say they want a lower price, but often other things such as service are more important and they are prepared to pay for it.

- **Keep on discounting with special offers:** you will educate your customers only to buy when you are on special offer.

- **Think in terms of "the price":** a single point pricing scheme is too simple for competitors to beat and for customers to compare. You need to be creative in how you price.

MARKET RESEARCH

You can use research for three basic reasons:

- Gain an insight
- Understand attitudes and behavior
- Track performance

Each requirement needs a different approach, as follows.

Gain insight

You can gain customer insight in plenty of ways:

- **Become a customer yourself** and endure the misery or delight your company creates. This is useful as a wake up call. But it is also dangerous. The experience of one executive, especially the chief executive, should never be used to represent the experience of the market overall.

- **Co-create products with your customers.** Your heaviest users are very useful: they often find creative and original ways of using your product and can see many more ways in which your products and services can be improved. Involve them directly in helping design the next generation of your products and you will have a product or service which you know meets the needs of the market.

- **Commission focus groups.** These are powerful and often misused. Executives often ask, "What did the focus group prefer?" That is irrelevant. You are not looking for a statistically irrelevant conclusion from a group of eight customers. You are looking for the one insight about how they really think about you and your rivals, about how they use your product or service in practice, what annoys them most about the service, and what they would like instead. Given you are looking for insight, it is often worth listening to the entire focus group yourself: do not expect the moderator to hear what you need to hear.

Understand attitudes and behaviors

This is the staple of many market researchers. Ask 1,000 people why they buy Ariel instead of Daz and then summarize the statistically significant conclusions. The problem with this is that customers will lie to you out of politeness and ignorance. They will say what they think they ought to say ("it was cheaper or better") not what you need to hear ("bought it because my dog likes its smell..."). Attitudes are very dangerous.

If you can, focus on behavior. Find out how people buy, how people decide. Choice is not always rational. In theory, you bought that mobile phone package because it was the best overall deal. In practice, perhaps you became overwhelmed by the confusing choice and in the end you bought because you trusted the knowledgeable sales person who gave you a good story to tell your friends about what a good deal you got. And the phone looks cooler than your colleagues'. So should the phone firm focus on price and benefits (the result of looking at attitudes) or focus on in-store sales support and product design (result of focusing on behaviors)? You need both.

look for the outliers and distinct market segments

With this sort of research, ignore the averages. Look for the outliers and distinct market segments: this is where you can build a distinctive offering and, hopefully, build a competitive advantage over less differentiated rivals.

Track performance

Tracking performance is basic housekeeping; for instance, consider:

- Market share
- Relative pricing
- Media spend versus competition
- Brand awareness, prompted and unprompted

This will not generate any great insight, unless you are doing a test market in one region which you want to compare with other regions. But if you fail to track it, you are leading the organization as blindly as if you had no financial information on performance.

COMPETITIVE AND MARKET INTELLIGENCE

You need to know about competition. Some, but not all of the answers are on Google. You need a little more work and creativity to find out exactly what you want to find out. Here are 10 ways you can find the answers.

Ten ways to find the answers

1   **Google.** Yes, Google, Facebook and other online resources will be a mine of information. The job of the intelligence analyst is not to find some dark secret, but to put all the pieces of the jigsaw together and build the big picture. Dig for press releases, speeches by key executives, comment, industry analysis, and more.

2   **Company accounts.** Companies are required to disclose more and more. Most people ignore the detailed findings because they are eye-wateringly boring. But in amidst all the routine rubbish there is always a rich vein of intelligence: mine that vein. And while you are doing this, you might ask their PR department to put you on their mailing list for the company newsletter, which will brag about their brilliant plans. Wonderful.

3   **Planning, trademark, patent, and regulatory filings.** These give early warning of what your rivals intend to do. Make sure you have all of these filings tracked and analyzed on a regular basis.

4   **Suppliers.** You probably share some of the same suppliers. They will get advance warning of new products and initiatives being planned because they will have to change what they sell to your competitor. They will be discreet, but try being nice to your supplier. You will be surprised what you can learn.

5   **Customers.** You probably also share customers who are more than happy to provoke you by telling you how much better your competitor is than you are, and how that competitor is going to introduce an even better promotion or product next year. Take the abuse, even encourage it. You want to find out all you can about your rivals as early as possible. Let your shared customers be your early warning radar system.

6   **Consultants.** They will never tell you that competitor X is doing Y. Instead they will show you an industry analysis which thinly disguises the same data. Or they will quote an industry example of best practice, which again will be your competitor thinly disguised. Let all the consultants show off their knowledge and learn from them.

7   **Ex-employees.** Most industries are fairly incestuous and you will probably have hired a few employees from your rivals. Make sure you debrief new hires thoroughly: they probably know more than they realize, and will tell you more than they intend even if they think they are being discreet.

8   **Industry sources.** Industry associations have plenty of information: use it. Brokers do industry and company analysis: they need to be nice to you, so make sure you get early copies of all of their reports. Be creative about industry sources. Media associations will tell you how much is being spent on different sorts of media by your industry: from there you can work out whether you are investing more or less than the competition.

9   **Mystery shoppers.** Buy your rivals' products and services. Experience what they are really like. And do not buy your own products and services through the special company scheme, because you will never endure the frustration and anger your firm forces onto your customers.

10 **Market research.** Most markets are already well researched. If necessary, commission some market research to find out what your customers really think of your rivals and why they do or do not use them.

If this sort of information is important on a regular basis, create a small competitive intelligence unit which can gather together all the titbits of information from sales people, buyers, customers, the media, and regulatory sources. Let them build the complete picture for you.

If you hire consultants at vast expense to do a deep industry and competitor analysis, they will give you the results of the 10 searches above. Most of them you can do yourself at no cost. A few of them require modest spending on market research or regulatory tracking. If you learn to do it yourself, you can keep yourself constantly up-to-date with your competitive intelligence, instead of relying on occasional and expensive ad hoc analysis by consulting firms.

WHAT PEOPLE BUY AND WHY

If you want to market your product or service, it helps to know why people buy. What you think you sell and what people hope to buy may not be the same thing.

Your product or service works at three levels for the customer:

- Features
- Benefits
- Hopes and dreams

Some highly simplified examples will make the point. First, off-road cars. They are curious because the vast majority rarely, if ever, go off-road. They are city cars. So the main benefit of the car (going off-road) seems pointless, until you look at what the manufacturers advertise. They advertise a dream, a self-image which appeals to a certain sort of city dweller.

Features	Benefits	Hopes and dreams
6.0 litre engine	Power	Be macho
Four-wheel drive	Goes off-road	Be the adventurer
High driving position	Safe	Save the kids and look down on everyone else

Second, a graduate recruiting proposition. Teach First attracts top graduates (over 7% of Oxford and Cambridge graduates apply every year) to teach in tough schools for two years for half the salary and twice the grief of working in a bank or consulting firm. So why does it work?

Features	Benefits	Hopes and dreams
Teach in a challenging school	Raise levels of achievement and aspiration	Fulfil personal ambition to make a difference
Over 1,000 top graduates	Mutual support and help	Have fun; build your network
Leadership training course	Backed by top employers	Fast start your career of choice

As a manager, the fatal trap is to fall in love with your own product. We get so excited about the amazing features of our product that we lose sight of what the customer is looking for. Even cleaning products have hopes and dreams, about being house proud. Selling Fairy Liquid in Scotland, I found working class homes all put their bottle of Fairy Liquid on a shelf in the kitchen window, where everyone could see it. Bizarre Scottish habit? No. Fairy Liquid is the premium detergent, and so it was a simple way of saying, for a few pennies extra, that the home maker had high standards and was house proud. The families with own label detergent carefully hid their product away in a kitchen cupboard, to avoid the shame of being seen to be penny pinchers.

the fatal trap is to fall in love with your own product

At the other end of the scale, cosmetics are sold purely on the basis of forlorn hopes and dreams: buy our product and look young, beautiful, and glamorous. Just like the car manufacturer or Fairy Liquid, they will still refer to some of the features of the product, to give the consumer the reason why they can believe the product claims. For cosmetics, the feature is likely to be some exotic sounding ingredient which has been tested in some plausible way.

"Features, benefits, hopes and dreams" sounds obvious but it is not. Producers focus on features too much. And consumers will not tell you what their hopes and dreams are. Coca-Cola made the classic mistake of thinking of their product in terms of features and benefits: when they were being beaten by Pepsi's "taste challenge" they responded with an improved product. Mistake. They were not just selling sweet fizzy pop. They were selling a culture, a dream of America and an identity. The market research never told them that and they never thought of it themselves.

No one says they buy Fairy Liquid to keep up with their neighbors, but they do. Instead, they play the producer's game when they are asked why they buy: they start talking about the features of the product (it lasts longer and is mild on hands). So you need more than research and marketing by the numbers to market well: you need creativity and insight.

HOW NOT TO SELL

Everyone needs to sell. The more senior you become, the more important sell-ing becomes. In some businesses this is explicit: you cannot be a partner in a consulting firm unless you can sell to clients. But even if you are not selling to clients, you have to sell your ideas and your agenda to colleagues.

The road to enlightenment is through failure, especially when it comes to selling. You can be taught all the theory, but it is only by messing up in front of clients that you learn, the hard way, what really works and what does not. So let us set aside the theory for a moment and learn how to mess up. If this saves you even one painful experience, it is worth it.

Think back to occasions when you have been thinking about buying but you did not. What put you off buying from that sales person? Here are some of the reasons I found when I have been buying:

- The salesman talked at me and did not listen.

- The salesman talked about his product rather than asking questions about me and my needs.

- I was given no space.

- He was more interested in making commission than in helping me.

- He gave me hype, not facts.

- He said trust me: never trust anyone who says "trust me."

- I got confused by too much choice: the greater the choice, the less the chance of finding the best package. I did not want to look like a fool to my family by getting the second best deal.

Ultimately, people do not buy because there is too much risk and uncertainty. Buying is stressful. Imagine buying the office photocopier: get it wrong and everyone will give you grief every time there is a problem. From this, we can start to see some of the basics of successful selling. Selling is partly about prod-ucts, but mainly about people. So it is as much an emotional journey as it is a rational one. The 10 basics of selling are shown on the next page.

None of these has anything to do with learning 25 different ways to close a sale. Most sales are not won and lost by learning fancy techniques. They are won or lost using the 10 principles on the next page: on the many occasions I have messed up it is because I have missed one of these 10 principles.

The 10 basics of selling

1   Listen.

2   Help more than you sell.

3   Focus on the client's needs, not on your product.

4   Be expert, but don't talk down.

5   Give the client time and space.

6   Offer a restricted choice of one or two options: simplify the decision.

7   Focus on the benefits of the product to the customer, not on its features.

8   Build trust, but never say "trust me."

9   Be positive and enthusiastic.

10 Give the customer a story which they can tell their friends and colleagues to show that they have made a smart purchase.

3

Finance and accounting

INTRODUCTION

Some people fall in love with numbers for the same reason people fall in love with distressed donkeys: they are preferable to humans. But numbers are very dangerous. They give the illusion of certainty in a very uncertain world. You cannot run a business just by sitting behind your desk and dealing with the numbers. John le Carré wrote in *Tinker, Tailor, Soldier, Spy*, "A desk is a dangerous place from which to view the world." That is as true for managers as it was for le Carré's spies.

numbers should support thinking, not constrain it

The good news about finance and accounting is that you do not need to be in love with the numbers: you do not have to be a math wizard. The key to working the numbers is to:

● Understand the business

● Understand the thinking and assumptions behind the numbers

● Understand why the numbers may or may not be reliable

If you can do this, then you will be highly effective at dealing with finance, accounting, and the math of the business. So the focus of this chapter is not on numeracy but on thinking. If you think clearly, you will be far more effective than someone who uses numeracy as a substitute for thinking. Numbers should support thinking, not constrain it.

MATH FOR MANAGERS

Math make some people break out into a cold sweat, while others start drooling with excitement. An MBA course makes all managers sweat the numbers and the math. Here are 10 ways in which you can drive business thinking into the numbers you are presented with.

Ten ways to control the numbers

1 **Work the assumptions not the math.** You know that the spreadsheet in front of you will have been created from the bottom right-hand corner upward. People start with the answer and then create assumptions to fit the desired answer. You need to unpack the assumptions behind the spreadsheet. And if the assumptions are ➡

not clear in the spreadsheet, do not be bamboozled by complexity. Insist on seeing a simpler version that highlights the real assumptions and variables.

2 **Test the what-ifs.** Try different scenarios with different assumptions and see what happens to the projections. Let your spreadsheet do all the number crunching.

3 **Remember the sacred numbers and reject the silly ones.** You should know your business and your core numbers: staffing levels, key budget line items, etc. If you see numbers that look odd, they are odd. Check them against your sacred numbers to see if the basic inputs are right.

4 **Don't be seduced by the average (mean, mode, or median).** The average human being is 52% female and has slightly less than two eyes and two legs (go figure that). There is no such thing as the average human. From a business perspective, outliers and segments are much more interesting than averages: they tell you more about your business and its opportunities.

5 **Math is an aid to thinking, not a substitute for thinking.** The clear answer on the spreadsheet looks definitive, but it is not. Keep your business brain engaged. For instance, your analysis shows that lower prices lead to more sales and possibly higher profits with economies of scale; but perhaps they also cheapen the brand, get the customers used to lower prices, and invite competitive retaliation so you end up far worse off. Good math can be the enemy of good thinking.

6 **Compounding is the most powerful force in the universe** (if an unlikely statement attributed to Einstein is to be believed). If your business grows at 10% per annum, it will double in seven years and grow to be 128 times its current size in your glorious 50-year career. And if one of my ancestors had put $1 aside for me at the birth of Christ at a miserly 2% compound, I would now own the entire planet (about $200,000 million million in value). Never believe a trend will last forever.

7 **Understand causality:** is violence on TV a cause of violence in society, or is violence on TV caused by society's desire for action movies? Do happy employees cause firms to be successful, or do successful firms cause employees to be happy? The math will show that there is a relationship, but will not show which is the cause and which is the effect. How you decide determines how you act.

8 **Scale counts so think big.** How can I sell detergent for $3 when the required advertising costs $6 million, plus all the sales costs, overhead, and R&D before we

even start on producing the product and paying for the raw materials? If I sell 100 million units a year, I can afford all this and make a big profit. The same goes for selling phone calls for a few cents a minute or for many other businesses: scale changes everything.

9   **Model your business.** Every business has a simple financial model behind it: understand that and you understand how to make your business more profitable.

10 **Forget the advanced math and keep it simple.** Bayesian analysis and chi square distributions are taught at top business schools, but are rarely seen in the world of management. Math should not just analyze, it should persuade. An analysis that no one understands is not persuasive.

SURVIVING SPREADSHEETS

The secret is that you do not need to be good at numbers in order to be good at analyzing spreadsheets. You just need to know how the spreadsheet is constructed. All spreadsheets are constructed the same way, from the bottom right-hand corner backward. In other words, staff start with the answer you want and work back from that. If you expect a 15% return, you will find the spreadsheet delivers 15.4%; if you want a million dollar profit, the spreadsheet will predict $1.057 million. Whoever constructed the spreadsheet will have wanted to exceed the target return while avoiding a round number that looks too simple.

Armed with this knowledge, you can now analyze the spreadsheet successfully. There are three basic questions to ask:

● **The venture capitalist's question:** what is the track record of the person presenting the numbers? A B grade spreadsheet from a manager with an A+ track record is worth far more than an A+ spreadsheet from a manager with a B grade track record. The numbers are only as good as the person who stands behind them.

● **The banker's question:** what are the assumptions that lie behind the numbers? Subject every number to the "what if" test: growth rates, market share, costs, salaries, etc. Start with the big assumptions: assumptions about the costs of the coffee machine will not make or break the spreadsheet (unless your business is selling coffee machines).

- **The manager's question:** do I recognize these numbers? Every good manager will know the basic operating numbers of their business: margins, costs, growth and more. See if the numbers in the spreadsheet align with what you know to be the reality of your business.

If you get positive answers to all of the above, you are probably looking at a robust spreadsheet. By asking these questions you may also uncover some uncomfortable truths. Either way, you will be in severe danger of looking very smart, even if you are the sort of person who normally hates numbers.

THE FINANCIAL STRUCTURE OF THE FIRM

You are on your own when looking for practical and impartial advice on deciding what level of debt and equity your firm should have. The theory (Modigliani-Miller) looks mainly at the cost of different sorts of financing, but not at what is most suitable for your sort of business: lowest cost is not always the best value. Providers of finance are always biased in favor of the sort of funding they provide: debt or equity. In practice, your decision will be based slightly on cost and greatly on your risk appetite.

lowest cost is not always the best value

Put simply, businesses with high risk should not double up their risk by taking on more debt; lower risk businesses can cope with more debt.

Risk is not driven simply by your level of debt relative to equity and/or cash flow. Risk and leverage are driven by the following:

- **Financial leverage:** level of debt versus equity. The more debt you take on, the more volatile your results will be. In good times, you will look very good. In bad times you will be the first to go bust: this is a lesson learned by private equity groups during the credit crunch.

- **Operational leverage:** high fixed-cost businesses are highly sensitive to volume variations. Airlines have high fixed costs of financing and staffing which leads to very low marginal costs of carrying one extra passenger on each flight. Yield management becomes a vital survival tool for all airlines.

- **Business cycle sensitivity:** some businesses are highly insensitive to the cycle, like water utilities. Restaurant chains, which depend on discretionary spending, are very cyclical. This means their cash flows can be volatile: adding high levels of debt, which demands cash to pay the interest rates in bad times as well as good, simply adds another layer of risk to an already risky business. Utility companies have stable cash flows in good times and bad, so can (and do) take on much higher levels of debt.

- **Pensions and other fixed commitments:** these are hidden fixed costs for many businesses, and are becoming increasingly important as regulation requires firms to maintain adequate funding of their pension funds. They are effectively hidden debt that has first call on your cash flows. The greater these obligations, the more risky it is to use debt to finance your firm.

If you have high operational leverage and high business cycle sensitivity it makes little sense to double your bets by taking on lots of debt as well. Equally, if you have very predictable cash flows, then you can afford to load up with debt. This is what water utilities have done, and typically private equity houses like to buy businesses with stable cash flows.

When you decide the level of debt your firm takes on, ask two questions:

- How much funding do we require to fulfil our ambitions (and perhaps we can be self-funding)?

- What will happen if we take on debt and our more pessimistic planning scenarios occur? Look at the required banking covenants, and if you breach them your bank will squeeze you for your last drop of blood. Banks are not paid to be nice. This is a basic financial risk assessment which tells you how much debt you can afford to take on. If there is too much risk, raise equity or scale back your ambitions and reduce your funding requirements.

MODELS OF BUSINESS

Behind every business there is a very simple financial model. Understand that model and you will understand what drives the business. Financial analysts will often try to capture performance in one simple metric; for instance, consider:

- **Retailers**: change in like-for-like sales (after the effect of new store openings and closures)—this captures the underlying health of the business

- **Subscription television**: average revenues per customer, and churn rate

- **Hotels**: occupancy and average revenue per room night

These are useful measures of the overall health of the business. As managers, it pays to go one step further and identify the specific levers that you can pull to improve the performance of the business. Three examples will help to make the point:

1 **Retailing.** The gross profit of a store is a result of five factors that can inform management decision making:

   a Number of people passing the store (location decisions)
   b Multiplied by the proportion of people entering the store (marketing decisions)
   c Multiplied by the number of people buying in the store (merchandising decisions and sales effectiveness)
   d Multiplied by the average value of each sale (merchandising and sales)
   e Multiplied by the average margin of each sale (buying and pricing decisions)

2 **Consulting.** This works on the basis of finders (partners who sell business), minders (managers who manage the business) and grinders (associates who do the work). The business model is then based on four variables:

   a Billing rates: how much you charge per hour, which varies for finders, minders and grinders
   b Utilization: how much billable time you expect from each level of the firm
   c Breadth of the pyramid: fewer finders means more leverage and more profit, but makes it harder to sell enough business
   d Rate of attrition and promotion: the faster you promote people, the faster you have to grow, or your pyramid goes awry. Alternatively, fire people in the middle and you create room for promotions from the bottom while keeping the shape of the pyramid and your economics together. New joiners do not understand the brutal economic reality that forces the up or out system of consulting firms

3 **Credit cards.** The credit card business depends on acquiring and keeping the right sort of customer. The simplified model of the business can be built around the value of each customer. The value of the customer is the result of:

   a The cost to acquire the customer: channel and marketing decisions
   b The average spend per customer: customer targeting, profiling, marketing
   c Average length of retention per customer: quality of service and operations

These are very crude ways of looking at your business. And that is the whole point. The simpler the system, the easier it is to see past the noise of day-to-day issues. Unless you manage the basic drivers of the business, the monthly variances appear as noise and you have to react to them on an ad hoc basis. Once you control the basic drivers of the business, you control its future.

FINANCIAL ACCOUNTING

Financial accounting is the bedrock on which the performance of the firm (and management bonuses) is based. Financial accounts should give a true and fair view of the financial position of the firm. In practice, most firms are proficient at managing the presentation of financial accounts, so that they are less of a bedrock of financial performance and more like quicksand in which you can easily sink.

Financial manipulation never improves the underlying performance of the firm. In most cases, it simply makes this year look good at the expense of future years. So bear in mind the following:

- As a manager, and potentially as an investor, it pays to read behind the headline numbers that are presented in the annual report and to understand the underlying performance of the firm. Here is what to look for: the exceptionals game. Many firms incur "exceptional" items every year: conveniently, these are removed from the headline P&L number. It is an easy way of boosting the reported P&L.

- Convert expenses into capital investment. Some capital investment is legitimate, like building a new factory. But some firms have happily capitalized marketing and IT spending on the basis that the benefit will be felt for years to come. Conveniently, that boosts profits this year and leaves a depreciation headache for your successor next year. M&A accounting is a law unto itself. There are two favorite tricks. First, buy a company with a lower PE (price to earnings) ratio than yours. Your earnings per share rise without any further effort on your part. Second, write off massive amounts of goodwill on the acquisition. This will be taken as an exceptional (see above) and will give you the chance to write back goodwill in later years if you want to boost profits later.

- Ignore impaired assets (like invoices which have no hope of ever being paid, or loans that will never be paid back to you). Keep them on the balance sheet, and avoid the expense of writing them off. Play the pensions game: take pension holidays when you can and then when you have to make extra payments to make up the shortfall, count them as exceptional.

- Aggressive revenue recognition. Deep discounts will pull sales forward from next year. Recognize as much of that $100 million project as revenue in this year as possible. One or two firms have resorted to illegal side deals with customers: taking stock today and letting them return it the day after the financial year closes. Thus revenues are recognized, but not achieved.

There is a long and ignoble roll call of dishonor when it comes to accounting trickery: Bernie Madoff, Enron, Lehman Brothers, WorldCom and Tyco are some of the more recent ones. You should be able to see through most of the smoke screens:

- **Read the notes:** they will show what is going on. If the disclosure documents are thick then something nasty may be hidden.

- **Reconstruct the cash flow statement**, from their balance sheets, for several years. This will tell you what is really happening with their sources and uses of funds.

- **Construct the pyramid of ratios** for the target firm for several years, and for its rivals. This will show whether underlying performance is improving or not.

HOW TO USE THE CAPITAL ASSET PRICING MODEL

The Capital Asset Pricing Model (CAPM) is one of the fundamental tools of the entire MBA course. It determines how much your project should earn to be viable, and helps you decide which projects are financially attractive and which are not. This is a critical tool. If you set your financial targets too high, you miss out on worthwhile projects. If you set the financial targets too low, you risk going out of business.

This section explores three ideas:

- How CAPM works in theory
- Why CAPM is dangerous in practice
- Why CAPM is unsound in theory

Subsequent sections look at practical alternatives to CAPM that managers can use day to day.

How CAPM works in theory

CAPM tells you that your investment (equity) needs to earn a minimum return, which will be the sum of:

- The risk-free rate you can earn on risk-free assets, such as government bonds issued by top quality sovereign borrowers

- A risk premium for investing in equities, which are inherently more risky than risk-free government bonds

- A risk weighting for the specific risk of your project, which may be more or less risky than investing in a typical equity

All of this is captured in a simple equation:

$$COE = R_f + \beta R_m$$

where:

- COE is the cost of equity.

- R_f is the risk-free rate.

- R_m is the risk premium on the market.

- β (beta) is the specific risk of the project.

So far, so good. It makes sense that the riskier the investment the greater the expected return should be. But this common sense falls in the face of management reality.

CAPM and management reality

CAPM contains three bear traps for the unwary manager: a project that is estimated to earn no more than the firm's target rate of return will probably fail. Managers who pitch projects are not paid to be pessimistic. They make the best case possible, and then hope that they (or more likely their successors) can deliver on their promises. So a project that promises a 10% return based on a manager's optimistic assumptions may struggle to break even. If the firm's CAPM target is 10%, you need to see a project that offers at least a 20% paper return: reality is rarely as rose tinted as the original proposal.

If all your firm's projects aim for the CAPM target rate of return, you will go bust. Any firm can be thought of as a portfolio of projects (call them brands, or businesses if you wish). Inevitably, some fail. Some meander along in a half life of hope. Others will be at an early stage of development and will be eating cash.

CAPM has nothing to say to mission driven firms

To pay for all these cash drains you need some parts of the business that earn vastly more than the target rate of return. These profit sanctuaries are essential to the survival of the business. You do not create profit sanctuaries by focusing on the target rate of return; you need excess profits wherever you can earn them.

Even if a project is financially attractive, it does not mean it is an attractive business proposition. The project has to fit with the business objectives of the firm. And CAPM has nothing to say to mission driven firms such as not-for-profit organizations, the armed forces, and much of the public sector where there is no profit objective.

CAPM is flawed as a theory

Look at the CAPM equation again:

$$COE = R_f + \beta R_m$$

Each part of the equation is problematic.

- The risk-free rate (R_f) is fairly harmless, although it makes a difference if you use the one-year or 10-year rate of return (between about 1% and 4%). And if you are based in a country with a financially weak government (currently Ireland or Iceland for example), you will find it hard to establish a sensible risk-free rate: your government's bonds will already carry a potentially large risk premium to cover the possibility of default.

- The risk premium (R_m) on the market is the stuff of fiction. Historic estimates vary between 5% and 9%, but even these ignore survivor bias. They are based on the long-run average of the UK and US markets. If you had invested in Chinese, Russian, or German markets in the last century, you could have experienced a 100% wipeout. If you had invested in Japan in 1990, you would have lost 75% of your money over 20 years. As an alternative, the forecast risk premium produces a figure of nearer 2%.

- Beta for most investable stocks is around 0.5 to 2, at most. But these stocks are already diversified portfolios of income streams. Within a firm, an individual project can be given a beta of anything from 0.1 (the saving from switching to a lower cost supplier) to about 5 (for an investment in a completely new venture).

Now use the least demanding assumptions above and you can justify a required rate of return of about 3%. Use the most demanding assumptions, and your rate of return shoots up to 50%. So you can use CAPM to justify a target rate of return of somewhere between 3% and 50%. You may as well stick a pin in a dartboard.

CAPM proves one of the eternal truths of management: good thinking beats good math every time.

ASSESSING INVESTMENTS IN PRACTICE

The simplest rule for managers is to work with whatever rules your firm provides. This is particulary true when it comes to pitching for investment. If your firm uses CAPM, use CAPM. If your firm uses another esoteric method, use that esoteric method, however good or bad it may be. Your job is not to change the system, but to work with it. In practice, that means making friends with the financial planning group early. They will jealousy guard their territory but don't fight them, work with them. The earlier you involve them, the more likely you are to succeed in adapting your proposal to suit their needs. Show you respect them and they are likely to be flattered to be treated as partners, not as obstacles. Make them into your allies, and they will start finding solutions for you, even as they are finding problems for your colleagues.

If you are in a position to make decisions about the required rate of return, you will need to do what most firms do: use some simple rules of thumb. These rules of thumb come with plenty of health warnings from finance professors. But in the world of management simplicity rules over sophistication. These rules of thumb will be targets that typically come in one of three flavors:

● **ROI (return on investment):** the higher the risk, the higher the expected return becomes.

● **NPV (net present value):** this is the discounted sum of all the cash flows associated with an investment. The riskier the investment, the higher is the required discount rate.

● **Payback period:** this looks at how many months or years it takes before the investment generates enough cash to pay back the initial investment. The higher the risk, the shorter the payback period required.

The simplest way of doing things is to sort all proposals into three piles: high, medium or low risk. High risk requires high returns, low risk requires lower returns, as follows:

● **High risk:** new products, new markets and new ventures.

● **Medium risk:** such as investment in new machinery and product extensions.

● **Low risk:** such projects may be dominated by cost savings (changing suppliers, cutting staff, changing the product mix).

This simple approach has the flaws of most approaches: it is open to game playing (what is high or medium risk?); it does not work for all sorts of spending (IT business cases are notoriously hard to connect to business and financial outcomes); and it only addresses the financial, not the business, case for a project. At the margin, some good projects will be missed and poor projects may slip through. But for the most part, business does not require making fine judgements about whether a project will make 10.1% ROI (accept it) or 9.95% (reject it).

To make a sensible investment decision, managers need to ask themselves four basic questions:

- Is the project financially attractive?
- Are the assumptions behind the proposal sound?
- Does the project fit with our strategy and direction?
- How credible are the people behind the proposal?

Ask these four questions and you are much more likely to make a good decision about a project than if you rely on CAPM.

NEGOTIATING YOUR BUDGET

Budgets are one of the must-fight and must-win battles of the management year. You have a choice:

- You can be an alpha manager and accept the challenging targets that your boss has dared you to rise to. That is a guarantee of 12 months of hard grind and frustration, with possibly no bonus at the end of the year as you struggle to hit an impossible target.
- Alternatively, you play hard ball and negotiate a sane budget that enables you to have a sane working year. You can then beat the modest budget and enjoy a bonus that your alpha colleagues will miss. Your choice.

Here is how to play budget hard ball.

How to play budget hard ball

- **Manage this year's performance.** If you overperform this year, you simply set a higher baseline for next year. Being a good manager, you should aim to beat the budget, but not too much. If you have slack this year, then delay recognition of revenues and bring forward recognition of costs where you can. This gives you the added bonus of a windfall start to next year: lower costs and quick sales against a modest target.

- **Set expectations low.** Find all the reasons why next year will be far tougher than this year: the market will be harder and the workload will be greater than ever. You know your unit better than anyone else, so you have the advantage here.

- **Strike early.** The later you leave it, the less room for negotiation you have. Starting early means starting before the formal planning or budget process has started. As soon as the first set of planning guidelines have been issued, expectations have been set and you have lost negotiating room.

- **Talk to the right people.** The right people are the decision makers and influencers: your boss, the CEO, and any planning group.

- **Be relentless.** Keep on hammering away with your analysis and your carefully selected facts. Eventually the planners will go away and search for easier victims.

- **Stay positive.** You need to be seen as the positive manager who will heroically overcome the daunting challenges which your unit faces. If there is any gloom, it is about external factors only. The outside world is the problem, you are the solution.

Of course, if you are setting budgets, then the rules are largely reversed. You have the advantage that you have seen all the game playing before and you have probably played the games before. You should also be reasonably familiar with the budgets, economics, and personalities behind each budget. As a budget setter, you need to apply five tests to each budget.

The five budget tests

1 **What are the key assumptions?** Numbers are simply reflections of assumptions, so test the assumptions not the numbers. This is routinely missed by managers who like to argue that the budget is too high or too low. That is an emotional debate that can only be defused by testing the key assumptions.

2 **How does this compare with last year?** This is where game playing becomes a real problem. But you should know the history of the unit and all its special circumstances, which you have had to adjust to. Newly appointed managers do not know this history and are most vulnerable to the game playing.

3 **What is happening in the market?** Budgets are by definition internal documents. Part of your job is to connect internal perceptions to external market reality. If sales and share are declining, then even HR and IT should take their share of the pain.

4 **Is productivity rising or falling?** Productivity measures the amount of work done for the amount of resource used. Even support functions such as HR and IT should be able to offer some measure of productivity. Inevitably, this will involve a degree of management judgement, but managers are paid to have and to use judgement.

5 **What is happening to unit costs?** Check the cost per unit: the cost per employee or the cost per tonne of raw material. Fight the inevitable inflationary assumptions which are built in.

MANAGING YOUR BUDGET

This is where prudence and practice part company, even though they share the same destination: you must make budget. Failure to do so is a career limiting move. Prudence and practice are two different routes to the same destination.

Prudence says you manage your budget conservatively. A simple rule is the 48/52 rule: aim to spend 48% of your budget and achieve 52% of your sales (or tasks) in the first half of the year. Once you have worked out what this means for the first half of the year, then apply the 48/52 rule again to the first two quarters of the year.

a simple rule is the 48/52 rule

The prudent approach means you give yourself a chance of beating budget. Just as important, it enables you to deal with any crises and unexpected events which may occur later in the year. You build in a safety margin into your operating performance.

The problem with the prudent approach is that it makes you a prime target for the year end squeeze, which comes around as regularly as Christmas but rarely brings any presents. The squeeze occurs because there are always some units that overspend or underdeliver: everyone has to be squeezed to make up the shortfall. By the time the year end looms, it is too late to make up ground in the marketplace, so the only realistic response to the squeeze is to cut costs. As ever, short-term savings can lead to long-term costs, so you need a way of insuring yourself against this.

The practical approach to managing budgets looks something like 51/53. You still want to get ahead on sales and outputs if possible. If you can achieve

53% of your goal in the first half, that is a good start. But you also need to find a way of protecting your spending. Since you know your budget will be squeezed in the last quarter, it makes sense to have no discretionary spending items left in the last quarter. In practice that means you have to spend ahead of the curve, selectively. That is not prudent, but within reason, it is practical. For instance:

- **Make essential investments early in the year.** These might be test markets, technology spend, market research and the like. Remove them from the coming squeeze.

- **Spend discretionary items which are dear to your heart early.** If you want a conference for all your units and team members, do not schedule it for the last quarter.

- **Commit budget where you can.** If you have advertising planned, make sure the media spend is committed. Advertising is a soft target for bosses who do not understand that cutting advertising kills your brand and your sales.

- **Build a slush fund.** Since you know there will be a squeeze, identify in advance where there is some fat to be cut. Simple acts such as delaying the start of new hires by a few months will allow you to build up reserves which can be released when necessary.

once the budget is set you have entered into a contract with your bosses

Finally, remember that once the budget is set you have entered into a contract with your bosses. You have to deliver on your commitment. Budget blues are the driver of much management angst, pressure and grief. Manage your budget tightly from day one and you have a chance of minimizing the grief at year end. If you are falling behind on budget, act swiftly. Cut fast to get your running rate of costs down: the longer you leave it, the greater the cumulative gap becomes and the less time you have to recover. The earlier you deal with your budget crisis, the smaller it is.

OVERSEEING BUDGETS

You will find very little written about how to control and oversee budgets which you have delegated down to managers beneath you. This is a vital art: if you cannot control the delegated budget, you will quickly find yourself in severe trouble. Here are six hard won lessons from the front line.

Six hard won lessons from the front line

1   **Be unreasonable.** There are always reasons why costs overshoot and revenue falls short. But if you accept excuses, you accept failure. If you see that budget might be missed, you simply have to focus on one question: "So what will you do differently to make budget?" These are uncomfortable but necessary discussions.

2   **The budget is the budget is the budget.** You will be asked to make budget revisions, which normally means reducing the budget. Don't. A budget is like a contract: your managers have promised to deliver certain results for certain resources: keep them to that promise.

3   **Cash versus accruals.** Cash is easy to spot: you have either spent the money or not. Accruals are the hidden iceberg that sinks many a budget. When reviewing a budget, make sure that you have identified every forward commitment, even if the purchase order has not been signed, and that it is reflected in the budget. You want to know about all the bad news as soon as possible, so that you can do something about it if required.

4   **Game playing.** As budget holders we are all used to playing games: hiding and deferring expenses (accruals) and bringing forward revenue recognition where we can. Perhaps we slip the start of a new promotion from the end of this year to the start of next year. Or we hire someone six months later than originally budgeted, which gives us a miraculous but unrepeatable cost saving in this year's budget. You are the poacher turned gamekeeper: you know the tricks, so stop them.

5   **Steal any cost savings.** If one of your departments makes a cost saving they will do their very best to spend the saving before you can do anything about it. Cost savings belong to you: they are your safety net for making up the inevitable shortfalls elsewhere. You will, of course, recognize and reward anyone who produces cost savings and you may even let them reinvest some of the savings in their area. But the decision is yours to make, not theirs.

6   **Work with your finance department, book keeper, or controller.** These people are your impartial financial ears and eyes. A good finance person knows the tricks, knows what to look for, and will spot problems before you do.

THE BALANCED SCORECARD

Financial and management accounts only give a partial view of the health of the firm. You need a more balanced view of performance that looks at how the firm is performing in the marketplace (share, sales); how it is doing organizationally (staff turnover, morale, etc.); and how well it is innovating. From this simple insight, Norton and Kaplan developed the idea of the balanced scorecard. As its name implies, it is an attempt to give managers a balanced view of the performance of their firm.

The balanced scorecard, however, is one of those good ideas whose time has come and gone. In the hands of the consultants, it just became too complicated and too expensive. Strip away the hype of balanced scorecards, and you can find a very simple and practical way of monitoring the progress of your business or department. Here is how:

Start with a blank piece of paper. On it, write down all the items of information you want about your business on a weekly and monthly basis. In practice, you will probably find that the information you want falls into five categories:

1 **Financial information.** You probably already have this, so this should be easy to fill in. But financial information is a lagging indicator of performance. It is best not to drive ahead by watching the rear view mirror. So you need some other sorts of information on your one piece of paper.

2 **Operations and business processes.** This answers the question, "What must we excel at, and are we excelling at it?" It covers the day-to-day performance of the business or department: are we executing on time, on quality, and efficiently?

3 **Market facing information.** This tells you how you appear to customers and competitors. How well are you serving your customers? Are you gaining or losing share? Where are you relative to competition? This is a current indicator and a future predictor of performance.

4 **Learning and growth.** This is your forward indicator of performance. Are you building new ideas, test marketing products, investing in change?

5 **People and staff.** How is our team doing? Are we building the right skills? Where are people on their career trajectory? Are we on top of compensation and performance management? How is morale?

I encourage managers to fit all of this onto one page of paper, because that reduces the data to what is most important. You remove the noise from the reporting detail. This is possible. P&G used to have a system where every brand had to produce a full report on the progress of its business on one side of paper. The type was small and filled the whole page, but if P&G can do it, most businesses should be able to.

The "true" balanced scorecard only has the first four categories outlined above. Bad managers focus only on the ideas and completely ignore the people (who sort of get covered in items 3 and 4 in their framework but are not explicitly headlined). Good managers realize that managing people is important.

Depending on the nature of your department or business, you will look for very different things in your one-page balanced scorecard. When you start, you will find that your existing reporting system gives you plenty of information which you do not need, and does not give you information you want. There will be blank space on your one-page balanced scorecard. You do not need all the information every day, week or month. For some things (such as staff morale) you might get a formal survey done just twice a year. Figure out what works for you, and slowly fill in the blanks.

If you are the CEO, cascade your one pager down through the organization. This tells the organization where your focus lies. And challenge your team to produce reports for their areas that are consistent with your one-page report: let them produce the detail which can roll up into your report. This can be done quickly and easily by you and the team without spending three months and $500,000 on consultants.

THE NATURE OF COSTS: CASH VERSUS ACCRUALS

George Orwell wrote: "Seeing what is in front of your nose requires constant struggle." The difference between cash and accruals accounting should be obvious, but it is regularly missed by some managers and routinely abused by others. So we need to explore the obvious and understand the impact that cash versus accruals accounting can have.

Cash accounting is simple: if I pay for something today I recognize the payment today. But what if I order something today, but I only have to pay for it next month or in the next financial year? In cash accounting, I would only recognize the payment when the cash left my hand next month or next year. But clearly, that does not give an accurate view of my position. I could run up huge debts on my credit card which, under cash accounting rules, I could ignore until the inevitable day of judgement arrived as the bill came through the mail box.

With accruals accounting, I recognize the debt as soon as I make the purchase, regardless of when payment falls due.

As with costs, so with revenues. Cash accounting will only recognize the revenue when the payment has been made. But if I have already done all the work and the client has agreed to pay 30 days after the bill is submitted, then cash accounting does not reflect my true position.

Accruals accounting gives a more honest picture of both revenues and costs than cash accounting. But inevitably, accruals accounting is subject to some discretion and judgement: at what point do we recognize revenues have been earned and will be paid? Just how big is our liability and what level of costs will we incur on all those extended warranties we sold last year?

Managers should treat accruals in the same way that auditors do: conservatively. Only recognize revenues when you are sure of them, and err on the side of safety in recognizing costs and liabilities. In the real world, surprises are rarely positive, so it makes sense for the accounting world to be cautious.

Not all managers see things this way. Many see accruals accounting as a chance to play games, especially near the year end. An easy way to make the year end target, when things are tight, is to be aggressive about recognizing revenues, and to defer recognition of costs until the start of the next year.

You have to decide which side of this game you are on. Accruals accounting gives you some scope to manage the appearance of your budget. But if you are monitoring the budget of other people, then it pays to dig hard and deep to understand just what has been recognized as costs and revenues, when they are being recognized and why.

THE NATURE OF COSTS: FIXED VERSUS VARIABLE

Much management time is spent looking at variable costs. Managers control variable costs because they are easy to see and easy to manage. In this respect a manager is like the drunk at night who lost his house keys in the woods, and so starts looking for them beneath the lamp post, because that is where he can see most easily. Occasionally we have to look into the dense woods of fixed costs if we want to improve our performance.

To make things simple: variable costs vary broadly with volume of output. Raw materials, ingredients, parts all vary with volume. The sandwich shop needs to buy more bread to sell more sandwiches. Fixed costs are fixed regardless of volume (more or less). Property rentals, overheads such HR, IT, legal costs do not increase each time the sandwich shop sells another sandwich.

Of course, no costs are fixed forever. If the sandwich shop grows, then it may need to take on more staff or even expand the shop and pay more rent. So "fixed" and "variable" are not absolute terms, but relative.

A few examples will show how fixed costs drive economies of scale, which lead to competitive advantage:

- **Marketing fixed costs.** If it costs $10 million a year to advertise a product effectively, then the market leader will just keep on winning. Work the math. Two detergents compete and both spend $10 million a year on advertising, both are priced the same and have the same production costs which give a 20% margin before advertising costs. Brand A sells $50 million a year and breaks even after advertising. Brand B sells $100 million a year and makes $10 million a year after advertising. Brand B can now always win: it has the room to increase advertising or reduce prices and Brand A cannot follow without losing money.

- **M&A and the fixed cost game.** Retail banking has been the subject of massive consolidation for the past 20 years, and it is nearly all about three types of fixed costs: IT costs, property costs (you do not need two branches next door to each other), and people costs (remove some branch staff and remove one set of head office and regional overhead costs). Revenues do not decrease because customers are more likely to change their spouse than their bank, even after a bank merger. So you end up with the same revenues but much lower costs and much improved profits.

- **R&D fixed costs.** These follow exactly the same logic as marketing fixed costs. If it costs $2 billion to develop a new car, or a new generation of computer chips, then the highest volume producer will make the most profit. They can then reinvest that in the next generation of cars or chips and the cycle continues until incompetence and complacency overwhelm the market leader, or a disruptive technology arrives.

The logic of fixed costs always helps the market leader over challengers.

The dark side

Fixed costs have a dark side. The first problem is leverage. Leverage looks very clever when things are going well, and looks pretty dumb when a recession or other setbacks hit. A typical example is an airline which has huge fixed costs that are not easy to turn off. A 747 that flies from London to New York costs nearly the same to run whether it is 5% full or 100% full. If the breakeven load is 75%, then each marginal passenger makes a huge difference, which means that yield management becomes a critical skill for all airlines. And if you own a fleet of 300 aircraft, then in boom times you may do well (provided other airlines do not add capacity to the market and spoil your party). In bad times, the fixed costs can sink the airline.

fixed costs have a dark side

The second problem of fixed costs is mis-pricing. Clearly, to make a profit the firm needs to cover both fixed and marginal costs. Together, these are the "fully loaded" costs of production. So the fully loaded cost of transporting a passenger from London to New York might be $1,000. But if you ignore the fixed costs of the airline, the marginal cost might only be $75 plus taxes: each extra passenger costs a tiny amount of fuel and some catering costs. All the flight attendants, for example, comprise a fixed cost which the airline is going to incur regardless of whether the extra passenger flies or not. So the temptation is to accept a passenger who only pays $100: the airline covers its marginal cost and makes a contribution to its overheads or fixed costs.

If it is only one passenger, it may make sense to charge only $100, even though the fully loaded cost is $1,000. But it rarely works out that way. Once each airline tries to fill its last few available seats at $100 each, the market becomes intensely price competitive and it becomes increasingly hard to charge the fully loaded costs of $1,000. The result is a massively unprofitable industry: globally, the airline industry has made a loss over the past 50 years. Blame it on the problem of fixed versus variable costs.

High fixed costs make a business very revenue sensitive: the good times become great times and the bad times become a nightmare.

CUTTING COSTS: METHOD CHANGES

Method changes are cost cuts as they should be: you find a different way of getting to the same outcome at lower costs. You change your method. Method changes may involve increased costs in the short term to deliver lower long-term costs. Investment in new technology, the costs of making people redundant and other short-term costs will lead to the notorious J-curve: you promise short-term pain (the downward part of the J-curve leading to lower profits) before costs go down and profits go up (the upward part of the J-curve). Managers are normally very good at delivering on the downward part of the J-curve: the upward part of the J-curve is less reliable.

Re-engineering is a classic form of method change. For example:

1 **Eliminate waste.** Waste comes in the form of:
   - Low quality leading to rework.
   - Delays and downtime, not just on the production line but in offices (decision-making delays, for instance) and in the supply chain (deliveries, etc.).
   - Unnecessary activities: duplication of work, re-entering data, activities which add no value. This is the rationale for much M&A activity: two firms together find that they do not need two sets of head office, HR, IT

infrastructure. Banks can eliminate overlapping branches and eliminate one set of IT costs; pharmaceutical companies can often eliminate one, very expensive, sales force.

2 **Find someone else to do the work** cheaper and better, for instance:

● Change suppliers.

● Outsource work: shift production to low-cost countries, IT and business processes to outsourcing specialists, including security, catering, payroll, property management, etc. This would make Adam Smith proud: it is the triumph of specialization which makes capitalism work best.

● Change the profile of your team. All teams become more expensive over time as people become more senior, so the cost of production goes up. Good managers manage this by moving senior and expensive team members up, sideways or out and then replacing them with cheaper and more junior staff. This is basic housekeeping.

● Find a way of achieving the same result cheaper: for instance, changing the media mix in advertising to target customers better and reduce your cost of customer acquisition, or changing your product's packaging.

● Make the customers do the work: call it self-service and "putting the customer in control" (e.g. self-checkout at supermarkets, online help for your software problems). True method changes should improve the customer experience: self-service rarely achieves this.

3 **Automate tasks.** From the production line to office productivity and IT tools, an ever wider range of tasks can be automated. The problem is that they do not always lead to cost reductions. Automating an inefficient and ineffective process is simply paving the cow path: you need to change the underlying way you do things to make the most of technology. Within the office, most office productivity tools do not reduce costs: they raise expectations. For instance, presentations used to be short, simple, and straight to the point until PowerPoint came along. Now that anyone can produce a 300-page PowerPoint presentation, that is what is expected. Costs, if anything, have shot up dramatically as highly paid managers waste their time trying to be PowerPoint experts.

There are two main approaches to method changes. The Japanese have an expression, "Open the back door, close the front door": slowly reduce staff levels through natural wastage as method changes take hold and productivity rises. This is fairly painless and is associated with *kaizen* and other continual improvement approaches.

The more traditional western method is the campaign approach, often led by the hero in a hurry to make their reputation. About every 18 months there is a new campaign: quality, putting customers first, service, and then eventually costs. The campaign approach might lead to a 20% reduction in costs once every five years; the *kaizen* approach might reduce costs 5% steadily every year. *Kaizen* is more effective and less painful. Campaigns produce heroes. So expect to see many more campaigns.

CUTTING COSTS: SLASH AND BURN

Method changes are elegant, but business is not always elegant. Sometimes you have to act ugly to achieve your ends. Cutting costs is rarely nice, but is often necessary. There is a natural hierarchy of cost cutting which depends on the degree of pain and the urgency of the need within the organization. The normal goal is to reduce costs without having to move to formal redundancies. The problem with redundancies is that they are high cost, and you lose the best talent because only the people who can move are ready to leave.

sometimes you have to act ugly to achieve your ends

The hierarchy, from least painful to most painful, goes like this:

1 **Eliminate discretionary spending.** Within this there is a mini-hierarchy: discretionary spend can include soft targets such as the coffee machine, flowers, and entertaining. Then cancel the year end conference and cut first or business class travel. These cuts cause grumbling, but nothing worse. Occasionally, items such as advertising and other marketing spend are seen as discretionary. They are good ways of cutting costs today and cutting revenues tomorrow, which makes things even worse in the long term.

2 **Cut back on marginal labor:** reduce consulting budgets (pain free to the organization). Eliminate overtime and outside contractors.

3 **Reduce total working hours:** ask for volunteers to move to flextime and part-time working.

4 **Extend the scheduled factory shut down** over Christmas or summer: you may still pay the labor costs, but most of the other costs go and you can reduce inventory.

5 **Ask for voluntary redundancies**, recognizing that often the wrong people volunteer. The best talent can go, the least talented are too fearful of finding new employment to move on.

6 Accept the inevitable and make compulsory redundancies: by this stage it is best to cut hard and fast. Minimize the uncertainty. Think of it as surgery without anaesthetic: cutting slowly is not a good way to do it. Work like surgeons in the Royal Navy in the days before anaesthetics: the best surgeon was the one who cut fastest.

Parallel to these efforts, firms may also try to slash and burn the costs of making and selling their products and services, which may include any or all of the following:

● Reducing product size

● Reducing product quality (cheaper ingredients, etc.)

● Charging for ancillary services, which used to be included in the price before (for instance, airline booking charges, check-in charges, baggage charges, security charges, seat allocation charges)

● Cutting selling costs by reducing sales and marketing budgets

These market facing slash and burn tactics may work in the short term. In the long term, they simply make the problem worse if they cause loss of market share or revenues.

CUTTING COSTS: SMOKE AND MIRRORS

There are endless variations of this game. Even the finance director, who normally acts as the sheriff, becomes a cowboy when it comes to managing the apparent costs (and profits) of the firm. Underlying performance is not affected, but the presentation of the results can be manipulated to meet your required goal. A few of the finance director's favorite tricks are:

● Make provision for "exceptional" items which happen to occur every year: this can appear after your headline profit figure, which is the one you hope investors will remember.

● Work the recognition of costs and revenues so that you can hit your targets as closely as possible.

● Take a pensions contribution holiday: bank the savings and leave the mess to the next person.

- Delay work on major expenditures, from advertising through to IT and beyond.

- Manage working capital tightly at year end to make your cash position look as flattering as possible.

- Improve the apparent cash position: leasing, sale, and lease back arrangements prevent you spending cash today.

- Move liabilities off balance sheet.

Within the firm, managers have to play this game to make their numbers.

Simple ways of making the numbers

- Renegotiate transfer prices between divisions: you win, your colleagues lose and there is no difference to the firm overall.

- Start charging for services which were previously free (this is a favorite of head offices to make their costs disappear: they "sell" their mandatory services to the operating units).

- Follow the finance director and manage year end cash positions tightly; defer or accelerate recognition of revenues and costs depending on your performance requirements.

- Delay or accelerate major expenditures so that they fall on the right side of the year end for you.

- Cost avoidance: show that you avoided a cost increase. This gets into "red dollar" syndrome. Unlike green dollars, which are real, red dollars are entirely notional. But they are a good way of showing that you are making an effort.

Purists will point out that this exercise is pointless because it makes no difference to the underlying performance of the business. It may be pointless for the business, but it is 100% relevant to the career survival and prospects of individual managers from the CEO downward. So it pays to learn how much flexibility you have in your budget, and then use that flexibility to your advantage. If you are over-performing this year, then you normally have everything to gain from avoiding too much over-performance. If you over-perform, your target for next year will be increased. Instead, bring forward recognition of costs and delay recognition of revenues: your target for next year will not be increased, and you will start next year with great revenues and low costs. Next year then becomes easy.

4

Human capital

INTRODUCTION

Firms like to say, "People are our most important asset." But in too many firms, loyalty is a one-way street: you have to be loyal to the firm which will be loyal to you for as long as it is convenient. And yet the underlying sentiment holds true: people make the business succeed or fail. As a manager, you will have responsibility for making sure that your own team stays in the performance zone: above the comfort zone but beneath the stress-out and burn-out zone.

Across the organization, there is a much greater challenge: how do you help everyone stay in the performance zone while maintaining the economics of the business and respecting the career ambitions and development needs of all your staff? Inevitably, you cannot achieve all of these objectives: if you have 5,000 people wanting to become CEO, you will end up with many disappointed people.

This is where the role of HR (Human Resources) becomes important. The HR function has endless different names, but a common purpose: make the most of our people. How this works varies by type of organization, but the principles remain the same. The purpose of this chapter is to explore the principles behind making the most of your people.

DEALING WITH HR PROFESSIONALS

In the past, firms used to have a personnel department that looked after matters to do with personnel. Nowadays we have the strategic human capital division. So what do they do? Look after matters to do with personnel. Whatever they call themselves, treat them well. Managers do not need enemies, let alone ones in the HR department.

People matters fall into two categories: operational and strategic.

Operational matters include things like payroll, employment law and regulations, and are normally outsourced to payroll firms, accountants, and lawyers.

Strategic matters are the ones to which managers and HR have to pay attention. There are three strategic goals for any staff strategy:

- Minimize the cost of production
- Maximize the quality of production
- Enable growth (and occasionally enable downsizing)

Inevitably, these three goals are often in conflict, and different parts of the firm will be pulling in different directions, so HR has an important job to do.

You will find that every three years or so, all the HR strategies will change: you will find that there is a new way of recruiting, evaluating, and developing people which is much better than the old way. This three-year cycle is driven by the average length of service of the HR chief: every time they are replaced, then all the policies will change as well, so that the new chief can show that they are different and better than the past. This means you gain zero mileage by challenging the way HR do things: they will be highly protective of their territory and it will change anyway without your intervention. Work with their system, not against it. HR are useful allies and dangerous enemies.

HR are useful allies and dangerous enemies

HR STRATEGY AND MINIMIZING THE COST OF PRODUCTION

In any firm, the cost of production naturally goes up. Staff want more pay. They want promotions which make them even more expensive. And to prove that they have big jobs to justify their titles, managers seek to employ more staff and increase their territory. This is as true of a consulting firm as it is of a manufacturing firm. If anything, it is worse in a consulting firm, because all the big egos think that they deserve immediate promotion, which would wreck the economic model of the firm if everyone's wish was granted.

Managers need to measure the cost of production across the firm and in every department. Staff departments in particular hate this, because they say that you cannot measure the productivity of lawyers or people in HR. Oh yes you can: you can always find measures of productivity. If nothing else, you can measure each department's costs as a share of revenues or overheads, and headcount as a share of total staff. They may be imperfect measures, but unless the department can find a better measure, use that one.

The obvious way to control the cost of production is to control headcount. Most firms do this reasonably well. The big strategic decisions here include outsourcing, offshoring, bestshoring, and all the other euphemisms for firing people in expensive countries where their jobs can be done for a fraction of the price elsewhere in the world. At the heart of this is a truly strategic debate: "What are we best at doing and what can other people do?" For instance, Apple employs over 30,000 people in Asia, of whom less than 100 are direct employees. Apple's skill is not in making all its products, but in designing and marketing them. Everything else can be outsourced. Most firms are finding that there is less and less they need to do directly. This is a lesson first taught by Adam Smith observing the pin makers of Gloucester: specialization and the division of labor works.

The second method of control is wage inflation. Again, this is sufficiently obvious that it is fairly well controlled. The third way to control the cost of production is by controlling the staffing pyramid: this is usually done very poorly.

To be efficient, a firm needs a lean staffing pyramid. There are two ways to disaster. First, the top of the pyramid should be narrow, not wide: you do not want too many overpaid chiefs. Second, you want to avoid being bloated in the middle with too many staffers and middle managers. Both problems lead to excess cost and to politics, infighting, and indecision among all the managers and staffers. This happens because large organizations find it hard to fire senior people (think of the Civil Service): no one likes firing their friends and colleagues who they may have known for 20 years. And senior people, like consultants, are very good at showing that they are indispensable. So it is easier to fire one of the young and cheap receptionists, which does little to address the underlying problem.

To control the cost of production, you have to manage the staffing pyramid. In a healthy firm, that means shipping out expensive people at the top of the organization on a regular basis, and making room for less expensive junior people to take over. This has the virtue of opening the way for more promotions and leads to greater clarity and accountability at senior levels.

The irony of this is that HR are both the solution and the problem. HR are part of the solution because they can help you manage the staffing pyramid. They are also part of the problem because they are one of the many staff functions who are very good at justifying their existence and expanding their empire.

HR STRATEGY AND THE QUALITY OF PRODUCTION

In staffing terms, quality of production refers only to the quality of the core input: people. You can do three things to manage this sort of quality:

- Recruit the right people

- Develop your people well

- Put them in the right positions

Recruit the right people

It pays to hire the right people. In one 18-month period I managed to fill the financial controller's role first with an idiot, then with someone who got caught trying to defraud us before I finally hired someone who turned out to be a drug dealer and armed robber on the side. It was expensive amusement. And the cost of staff turnover is high: each time a post has to be filled, assume that it will cost you 50% to 100% of annual salary to fill that position once you have allowed for head hunters, advertising and interviewing expenses, costs of laying off the hiring error, and then the cost of finding a temporary replacement.

Every HR group has its own theory about the right recruitment methods. In France, the use of graphology is widespread. In Anglo-Saxon countries, aptitude tests and psychographic profiling are common.

Live with the current orthodoxy: you probably have better things to do than to argue with HR professionals about recruitment theory. Instead, look at why people get hired and why they get fired. Broadly speaking people get hired for three reasons, in order:

- Proven technical skills

- Proven track record

- Other: fit, psychographic profile, attitude, hunger for the job, age, and sex (although do not admit that, ever)

Now look at why most people get fired:

- People skills, or lack of them

- Values

- Other: gross incompetence (rare), disloyalty to the boss, being an armed robber on the side

In other words, your recruitment process will probably do a decent job of finding out if your hire has reasonable technical skills and track record: most recruiters like to recruit someone who has done the job before.

Where you need to focus your efforts is in two areas:

- Does this person have good interpersonal skills?

- Will this person fit with the values we have?

you can train people in the right skills, but not into the right attitude

Try using the method which the shoe repair chain Timpson used for recruiting people to work in its shoe repair shops. Employees usually worked with little supervision and even less pay. And yet they dealt with customers all day. Timpson quickly found that recruiting to skills (mending shoes) was a disaster. What was needed were people with the right attitude: you can train people in the right skills, but not into the right attitude. So Timpson issued all area managers with a series of cards with Mr. Men cartoons on them. If any potential recruit was seen as Mr. Lazy, Mr. Fib or Mr. Slow, they were not hired. If they were seen to be Mr. Helpful, Mr. Honest, Mr. Speedy, or Mr. Positive, they might get in. It did not do well on gender diversity, but it did very well on recruiting the right sorts of people.

Timpson's approach may not be as clever as your HR department's latest psychographic profiling system, but it runs the risk that it might actually work in practice.

Develop your people

Management training has a bad name. This is a surprise since many executives will spend over $60,000 of their own money on management training: this is what an MBA is. Training is one of the first items to be cut when budgets are tight.

The CIPD (Chartered Institute of Personnel Development) did a study to find out what the obstacles to training were. Here are the top five replies:

- Not enough time

- Pressure of work

- Personal commitments

- Boss would not let me go

- No culture of training

Perhaps it is worth giving a little translation to these findings:

- Not enough time (not a priority for me)

- Pressure of work (still not a priority for me)

- Personal commitments (it really is not a priority for me)

- Boss would not let me go (not a priority for my boss either)

- No culture of training (in fact, not a priority for anyone)

So why will people pay $60,000 for an MBA but not attend free training provided by their own firm? There are three problems:

- Most training is perceived to be remedial, so it is an insult to be asked to go on the course. If you go on a leadership course, the implication is that you are not a good leader; you go on an interpersonal skills course or time management course because you are lousy at dealing with people or time. At least, that is the perception, even if it is not the intention.

● Too many trainers are not up to the job. Once you have sat through two days of watching a facilitator with a flip chart and a franchised theory asking you to guess what they are going to write on the flip chart, the instinctive reaction is to discover your inner axe-wielding maniac.

● Even if the trainer is good, the training is either not relevant or not practical. Managers want ideas that they can apply now, and they want immediate solutions to today's problem. So learning about interpersonal styles and doing MBTI (Myers Briggs Type Indicators®) is interesting but not of immediate use. It takes too long to master the clever theory, and it is not clear how it will help me with the fact that my project is two weeks overdue and the month end accounts look dodgy.

The many problems with training give some clues as to what you can do about it. And you have to do something: if you are not developing your team, you are not managing them well.

Developing your team

1 You are the number one trainer for the team. By coaching each team member well, you give them the real time support and advice they need. And the advice is credible, because it has to stand the practicality test: they have to go and apply the idea immediately and you both have to hope that it works.

2 Your team is the number two training resource for the team. When you have team meetings, find time to allow sharing of best practice, problem solving, or having someone showcase how they achieved something. Again, this passes the tests of immediacy, relevance, and credibility. The solutions may not have academic integrity, but they have the virtue of practicality.

3 Make formal training events a privilege, not a requirement. Only allow a chosen few to go on training programs: let them compete for the few training dollars or days at your disposal. The people who go not only get two days away from the office: they get all the bragging rights in the office. Training should never be seen to be remedial.

4 Put your team in control of training. Do not tell them what courses they have to go on. Let each team member select. Some will make mistakes, but at least it will be their

mistakes. For the most part, they will select courses which are most relevant to their needs and which are best quality: different courses quickly establish a reputation for quality or otherwise.

5 Provide your team with an external perspective. If you are their number one trainer, you could really mess them up with those faults you never realized you have. So they need some counter-balance and independent advice, especially when it comes to tricky issues such as managing their boss. So let them have an external coach if they want one.

Put your people in the right positions

Although courses and MBAs are useful, most managers learn from experience. And this is where things go wrong. In management-speak, a "development opportunity" is a "crushing weakness." Bizarrely, managers think that the best way to deal with a development opportunity is to get the team member to focus on it. How many Olympic gold medalists won by focusing on their weaknesses? Make weightlifters focus on their synchronized swimming skills?

Most managers succeed by finding some things that they are very good at, and then working around their weaknesses. Some weaknesses, such as an inability to deal with people well, are terminal: no amount of training or development will get the dysfunctional sociopath to change.

As a manager you have to find the context in which your team members can succeed best. Right context has two contradictory elements:

● **Where your team members can showcase their existing skills and talents.** This allows them to perform well, but it also means that they can be caught in a comfort zone or imprisoned in a tight box of technical expertise. Having a skill in doing reconciliations in the tripartite asset collateralized repo market is valuable but it is not one with great prospects.

● **Where your team members can build skills for the future.** If they are to progress you need to identify what skills they need for their career in five years' time. Start building those skills now. You need to help your team members develop for tomorrow as well as helping them perform today.

Just as you do this for your team members, so you should apply the same principles to your own career management. Balance your need to find a position where you can perform today, with the need to build those skills which you will need in your future career as well.

HR STRATEGY: ENABLING GROWTH (OR DECLINE)

To manage in a growing company is to discover life in easy street. There are always plenty of opportunities and promotions to go around: if you miss one opportunity, another will come along shortly and might be even better. By contrast, if you're involved in crises and downsizing, this may not be easy street, but at least there is clarity about what needs to be done and you can get everyone focused on the task of survival. The really hard time to manage is in steady state: no one has a sense of crisis and they all want their promotions and bonuses, which are not there if you are not growing. So either the firm grows fat (which leads to the crisis) or the politics and dissatisfaction grow as expectations fail to meet opportunities in HR terms.

The key to growth and decline is that you do not simply do more or less of the same in the same way. You have to keep on changing the way you do things. In decline, it is obvious that you have to change the way you do things. It is easy to miss the need to change the way of working when you are growing: why not simply do more of the same?

As you grow, some economies of scale come naturally: for instance your advertising budget is supported by greater volumes. In HR terms, scale economies do not come naturally. In the dash for growth, it is too easy simply to add more bodies. As the firm grows, scale economies come from increasing job specialization: this helps both with quality and with productivity. For instance, the solo consultant is a Jack of all trades and probably master of none: they are even their own IT help desk, receivables management team, and administrative assistant. The largest consulting firms have specialists by function for each industry as well as an array of internal support functions: quality goes up and cost to deliver goes down.

in the dash for growth, it is too easy simply to add more bodies

In decline, the reverse works: reorganization leads to jobs being combined. In both growth and decline, the changing nature of each job means that you have to redefine roles, management processes, decision making, compensation: everything changes. In practice, firms that are managing decline do not have the luxury of redesigning their work and restructuring before they cut: they have to cut first, fast, and deep. The cuts are then the vehicle that forces the firm to discover, or rediscover, new ways of working.

HR STRATEGY: COMPENSATION

When was the last time one of your team members asked for a pay cut for the same amount of work? How often has someone asked if they can be demoted? And how many team members tell you that they are not much good at their job?

In the hands of compensation experts, compensation is an objective discipline: measure the size of the job, do some industry benchmark comparisons and you have the answer. This is a useful discipline: it tells you whether you are in the right pay league or not.

Compensation is an exercise in managing human nature, which can be very emotional when it comes to pay. Everyone on your team will want two outcomes from the pay settlement:

- **More money than last year**, so that they can fund an ever improving life style and gain some degree of peace at home: asking the family to cut back is not a pleasant experience

- **More money (especially bonus) than anyone else on the team**, so that they can get the bragging rights. To award someone a lower bonus than their colleagues is not just a statement about pay: it is like saying, "You are worth less as a human being than your colleagues (who you despise)."

You will rapidly find that compensation can demotivate more than it can motivate: even the city trader who earns a $200,000 bonus will throw his toys out of the stroller and resign (after banking his bonus) if he finds colleagues have gotten a $300,000 bonus. Big salaries go with big and very fragile egos.

Accurate compensation

To compensate accurately, you'll need to think about the following:

- Get the industry benchmark data: you need some way of having a rational discussion about an emotional subject.

- Set expectations early and low, and keep on reinforcing them. If you surprise people, surprise them on the upside, not on the downside.

- Keep salary and bonus settlements secret: unsubstantiated rumors about who got what are better than the reality. Reality is likely to show that at most one person won, and everyone else lost.

- If you want to motivate people, look beyond compensation. Recognition, praise, giving people a worthwhile job, showing you care, helping people develop their careers will go further than adding 10% to their salary. The army does this well: pay people little, but give lots of recognition with medals, and create a strong *esprit de corps*.

- Be prepared to pay above industry average to attract and keep the best performers. 80% of your problems come from 10% of your staff, and top quartile performers can be four times more productive than bottom quartile performers. And if you overpay, then your stars will find it hard to go to another job and improve on their salary. If you pay low and get low performers you achieve nothing.

- Don't believe that bonus schemes are mandatory. Where individual performance is everything (trading and sales) they make sense. Where team performance is everything, bonuses simply become divisive.

Finally, remember that no compensation discussion exists in a vacuum. For the individual, compensation should be linked to their development. For the firm, compensation should be linked to an understanding of the overall costs of production, the staffing pyramid, rates of promotion, and career management for all staff.

ORGANIZATION CULTURE AND WHAT YOU CAN DO ABOUT IT

You'll notice that there is a difference between the formal culture of a company, which is often expressed in a values statement, and the daily beliefs of that same organization. These daily beliefs are the rules of survival and success which people follow in reality. Often you can find a large gap between the formal beliefs and the daily beliefs of the organization.

As you dig deeper, you find most large organizations have radically different cultures in different groups: sales are different from R&D who are different from accounts. In banks, retail banking and investment banking live on different planets.

So what can you do about such cultural chaos and confusion? You can do two things:

- **Remember the words of Warren Buffett:** "I find that when a manager with a great reputation joins a firm with a lousy reputation, it is the reputation of the firm which remains intact." So find a firm which suits your style: if you are entrepreneurial, do not join a risk averse firm even if they are pleading with you to sprinkle your entrepreneurial pixie dust over them. It will be the marriage from hell, and you will not survive. You have to find the context in which you can thrive. Above all, that means you have to be happy signing up to the culture of the firm you will join.

- **Set the culture for your own team.** You will be remembered less for what you do and more for how you are. If you want to be remembered as the duplicitous and authoritarian politician from marketing, so be it. Your team will take their cues from you. Every time you walk into the office with your little cloud of gloom, it will soon spread like a major depression across the office. If you are Machiavellian and mean, do not expect your team to be open, trusting, and generous. How you behave determines how your team behaves. Your choice.

ORGANIZATION CULTURE AND HOW TO CHANGE IT

A good way to fail as a CEO is to start a culture change program: it is unlikely to succeed, and even if it does it will take too long and may (or may not) affect the results of your business.

Cultural change initiatives are set up to fail from before they start. Here is why:

- Cultural revolutions have a bad name: think Mao and 50 million dead. Or Pol Pot and the killing fields.

- An attack on the culture of a firm is, by definition, an attack on the majority of the staff and the way they work. Most people resent being told that the way they have worked for 20 years is rubbish.

- Cultural change means mindset change: my bosses can mess with my roles and responsibilities, but they will not mess with my mind, thank you very much.

And yet a dysfunctional culture leads to dysfunctional results, so can you walk by on the other side of the road and pretend there is no problem?

If you want to change the culture, do not attack it head on. You will lose. Attack it crab wise: from the side. As a leader, this is what you can do to change the culture of your firm without ever stating that intention:

Changing culture

- **Be a role model for the values you believe in**, and be consistent in how you act.

- **Recognize and celebrate people who do things in the new way:** support other positive role models. You do not need to say the old ways are bad, you simply let the new ways grow in their place.

- **Find some moments of truth to make your point:** where there is a tough decision, be guided by the values you believe in and make sure everyone knows that is why you took the decision you made. People believe what you do, not what you say.

- **Hire and fire according to the new values.** A few ritual executions of the old guard will concentrate everyone's minds wonderfully. Remember the old saying: to scare the monkey, kill a chicken. Make values an explicit part of the hiring criteria.

- **Change the compensation structure.** Pay drives behavior. If everyone is on an individual bonus, do not expect great teamwork. If you incentivize call center staff on the number of calls they handle, not on how well they handle the calls, do not expect great customer service. You get what you pay for.

- **Over-communicate.** Official communications such as the company newsletter have all the credibility of Pravda in the Soviet era. Few people read it and even fewer believe it. Hold town hall meetings, meet face to face, and explain what you are doing from a business perspective, not just a cultural perspective.

- **Be patient.** It will take time for everyone to work out the new rules of survival and success and to adapt. There will be game playing: people will change their face but not their minds. Be relentless and consistent in all that you do, so that eventually the new way of working becomes habit.

WHEN TO FIRE SOMEONE

Occasionally, an employee will commit spectacular career hara-kiri and they make the firing decision very simple. Like when I found our bookkeeper was not just trying to defraud us, but was also an armed robber in his spare time. Easy decision.

Mostly, the decision is tough because things are not so clear cut. The trick is to know if someone has hit a bump in the road or is in a vortex of doom. If they have hit a bump in the road, they will often come out of it stronger and wiser (at your expense) and will be a more valuable employee. Once they hit the vortex of doom, it is like a black hole: there is no known means of escape, although the slide to oblivion can be slow and ugly.

The difference is normally clear when you look at how they react to a setback.

	Bump in the road employee	Vortex of doom
Perspective	Forward looking, action focus	Looks back, analyzes
Responsibility	Takes ownership	Blames others
Way forward	Delivers on clear promises, fixes problem	Half-breaks half-promises and makes more excuses
Language	Clear, simple, direct	Evasive and convoluted

When someone is in the doom vortex, move fast. The longer you leave it, the more they will drag others down with them.

When performance heads south it is rarely because of a lack of technical skills: an accountant does not suddenly become incompetent overnight. Poor performance is normally the result of poor people skills and poor values, which make it difficult for the employee to get things done. This is important because most people are hired for their technical skills, but fired for their people skills and values. So if you want to avoid firing people, hire the right people: look at their people skills and values as much as you look at their technical skills.

if you want to avoid firing people, hire the right people

Finally, be careful that you are not part of the problem. If there is a performance problem, then as the manager you are ultimately accountable for that. If there is a values problem, it may be that the two of you simply have different styles and cannot get along. So find some impartial advice before blundering in and earning yourself a lawsuit and damages.

Of course, you do not have to fire them. You may be able to move them on to some other department and let them make the painful decision.

ETHICS

In most business schools the ethics course need only teach two things:

● Your ethics will be determined by your industry and your employer.

● Ethics is not about honesty and morality: it is much more important than that.

Your ethics will be determined by your choice of industry and employer

Some employers have high ethical standards, others require a more flexible approach to ethics. The defense industry works to one set of standards, medical practice works to another. The CEO of a reinsurance brokerage firm assured me: "If you want to get ahead in this business, you have to put your liver on the line." He was an alcoholic, and all his best brokers had very low golf handicaps. Understand the expectations and make your choice.

It would be nice to think we can keep separate standards from those of our employers. This is not the case: most of us rise or fall to the level of expectations and standards around us. The scandals which afflict the corporate world come largely because everyone bought into a way of doing things which seemed to make sense to the insiders, but then looked unacceptable when exposed to public scrutiny.

If you have high ethical standards, pick the right employer. If you are more flexible, there are plenty of firms which will be delighted to hire you.

Ethics is not about honesty and morality: it is much more important than that

Let's make this simple: do you want to work for a boss you do not trust? Do you want to deal with a contractor you do not trust? Occasionally we may have to work with people we do not trust, but where possible most people prefer to work with other people they feel they can trust. So the point about morality and ethics is not to save the world: it is to show that you are someone that can be trusted. If you are not trusted, you will find it hard to attract a team, hard to get the support of colleagues, and hard to get clients. You will be functionally useless.

Building trust takes time and consistent behavior. The three drivers of trust are:

- **Values alignment:** do we have the same interests, values and priorities? You have to show you care not just for your own interests, but that you understand and care for the interests of your client and your team. When you do this well, you will hear managers spouting the jargon, "We are all singing from the same hymn sheet, you certainly talk the talk...."

- **Credibility.** You have to deliver on what you say. You even have to deliver on what you do not say. If you fail to disagree with someone when they are in full flow, then they will assume that you have agreed with what they are saying: you will by default have agreed to their project, their promotion request, their delivery deadline. Be very clear and very consistent in what you say and what you do not say.

- **Moments of truth.** There are always difficult moments: these are the moments when you build or destroy trust. Broken trust is like a broken vase: very difficult to put back together again perfectly. Moments of truth are those awkward moments when you have to deal with the underperformance of a colleague, or you have to disappoint a client. If you handle these moments promptly and positively, you can build trust. Shade the truth or deny the problem and you lose credibility.

Ethics, honesty, and morality are all fine things, but for all managers the most precious commodity is trust.

5

Operations, technology, and change

INTRODUCTION

MBAs are useful, but it's important to remember that an MBA is a classic university discipline. It is good at transferring a body of explicit knowledge from one generation to the next but is very poor at dealing with tacit knowledge. (Tacit knowledge is all about the know-how skills, as opposed to explicit knowledge which is all about know-what skills.) So most MBA courses struggle with operations, technology, and change: these are more know-how skills than know-what skills. But as a manager, you need to be comfortable with these skills: even if you are not an operations expert, you need to know what questions to ask and to know what good looks like. And all managers have to master the mysteries of change: if you cannot change things, then you are an administrator, not a manager. So this chapter takes you beyond the comfort zone of the MBA and into the wilds of practical management.

HOW TO START A CHANGE EFFORT

Administrators manage a status quo. Managers improve things, which means that they need to make change happen. To manage is to make change, but most people do not like change. Change implies risk,

most people do not like change

uncertainty, and doubt. And the risk is not impersonal business risk but a personal risk: will I be able to adapt to the new ways? So you start your change program with a cheery smile and quickly find yourself caught in the quicksand of corporate politics. All the objections to your idea will be stated very rationally, but in many cases the rational objections hide people's personal fears. The more you deal with the rational objections, the less you deal with the real objections, which are personal. You find yourself going where most change programs go: nowhere.

So before you start your change program, you need to know if it is set up to succeed or fail. Generals believe most battles are won and lost before the first shot is fired. The same is true of change efforts: failure or success is determined even before you start.

Over many years, one formula has accurately predicted whether change is going to succeed or fail. The formula is called the change equation. Here it is:

$$N \times V \times S \times F > C$$

In plain English the equation states that change will succeed where a real Need for change (N) and a Vision of the change (V) with Support (S) combined with practical first steps (F) exceed the Costs and risks of the change (C).

Let's look at what each term of the equation means in practice. The key is that the equation is not just about the likelihood of changing the organization: it is also about the likelihood of individuals in your team supporting your change.

- **N**: what is the compelling need to change? What is the problem you are solving? If there is no need for change, you will find it very hard to build momentum to overcome the resistance to change. Smart managers often create the crisis to build the case for change: they show that the competition is about to eat your lunch, or that your existing market is under threat.

- **V**: Lay out a clear vision of the change: what will be different at the end and what are the benefits? For the company, financial benefits are top. For the individual, they need to see that they will have a role and can thrive as a result of the change. So make the vision personal to each individual. If you do not have a clear vision, then you will find lots of effort is dissipated as people try different things in an uncoordinated way.

- **S**: you need the power barons to support your change. Align your agenda with theirs: show that your change agenda will support them. Find a sponsor to guide you through the politics. Once you have support from the top, you will find it much easier to gain support from colleagues: you have just changed their personal risk equation. Now that you have top support, it becomes far more risky for colleagues to stand in the way of change. Beyond top support, you need a very good team supporting you on your change effort. Hold out for the A team, not the B team. If someone is an A player, they are unlikely to be available. So you will naturally be offered a team of people who are available: these will be the B players. As a rule, refuse anyone who is available. Poach the top team.

- **F**: you need some practical first steps to get the bandwagon rolling. Find some early wins that you can publicize: everyone likes to back a winner.

- **C**: the obvious costs of change are time and money. There are also obvious business risks which go with most change ideas. Take time to understand the personal agendas of each individual: work their personal risk/reward equation. If necessary, increase the perceived risk of doing nothing, so that change seems relatively more attractive.

Some 90% of the effort of a change program happens after the formal start; but success is perhaps 90% determined before the formal start. So invest heavily in setting up change to make it succeed. It is better to walk away from a poor set-up, than to commit to losing.

SETTING UP A PROJECT FOR SUCCESS

Traditionally, projects fail because they are killed by one of the four horsemen of project apocalypse. Deal with these horsemen, and you have a chance of succeeding.

1 **The wrong problem.** "42" is a great answer to "What is seven times six?," but it is a lousy answer to the question "What is the capital of Australia?" You cannot hope to succeed unless you are answering the right question. The right sort of problem in a firm has three characteristics:

   a It is important, not just to you, but to your boss, the CEO, and the firm as a whole. If it is not important, it will be ignored.

   b It is urgent. Lots of things are important, like global warming. But if the boss has a toothache, then it is clear what he will deal with first.

   c There is a significant prize to be gained from fixing the problem; ideally, it is a financially quantifiable prize. For many IT projects the prize is more basic: do this or you will not be in business in five years' time. That is an ugly but compelling piece of corporate blackmail. It always works.

2 **The wrong sponsor.** You probably have many things in your inbox that are both important and urgent. But these things may be unimportant to your boss or your CEO. If you are starting a project, you need to make sure it has strong support. A powerful sponsor will help you clear the inevitable road blocks that appear, can help you get the key approvals, and can broker deals when you need them. So your project has to be important not just to you but to people who have power in the organization: power to get budget, power to get the right team in place, and power to overcome political resistance. Without strong support, you will quickly find your project disappearing into a blind alley of irrelevance.

3 **The wrong team.** If you get the B team on your project, you have a recipe for sleepless nights, constant struggle, and disappointment. You need the A team if you are to succeed. This is what the A team looks like:

   ● Right mix of skills.
   ● Right attitude: positive, proactive, and good at dealing with people.
   ● Right experience: they understand that projects are different from business as usual.
   ● They will all be unavailable, because they are so good. That is why you need them, not the combination of the untried, unused, and unusable which you will be offered initially. If you get the B team, that is evidence you have a weak sponsor who cannot secure you the right team. Play hardball to get the right team and be prepared to walk away.

4 **The wrong process.** This is where the MBA is worthwhile as it will allow you to manage a project well. But if you have the right problem, right sponsor, and the right team then first of all you are unlikely to have the wrong process. And even if your process does go awry, you will have the talent and the support to get it back on track fast.

MANAGING PROJECTS

First, the good news. There are plenty of fully qualified project management practitioners out there who have mastered the 40 activities and seven work processes of formal project management. They can be hired at modest cost and will ensure that you comply with government requirements on project management.

The bad news with formal project management tools is that they become very process bound: once you have completed your risk log, issue log, meeting log, telephone log, master log, and activity log, you may find that you have not actually achieved anything.

Most managers have neither the time nor the need to become fully accredited project managers. And yet we always have to manage projects. So we need something simpler to guide us.

Here are the basic principles:

The basic principles of project management

1 **Start at the end.** This infuriates those who suggest "first things first." But if you simply do first things first, you'll end up in a random walk from today to the future. Be crystal clear about the end goal, and make sure that everyone else is just as clear. Focus the goal as far as possible. With a clear, focused end goal you can eliminate large amounts of peripheral activity and waste.

2 **Work back from the end** and identify the minimum number of steps required to get to the goal. Anyone can create complexity. As a project manager, part of your art is to create simplicity and focus. Within this, identify the critical path of must-hit dates. The critical path simply indicates that activity A has to happen before activity B can start: this gives you the "brick wall" dates which cannot be changed or moved. From this, you get even more focus.

3 **Break the project down into manageable, bite sized chunks.** "Reengineering the corporation" is too big for anyone. Break this down into more manageable work

streams, each with its own critical path, and each with its stream lead who can be held accountable for the progress of that workstream.

4   **Identify other pre-conditions of success and how you will manage them.** If you are working on a marketing project then IT and HR may not seem important, until you realize the sales force may need retraining and new incentives, supported by a new IT system. Make sure the project enablers are properly managed.

5   **Put in place simple governance.** This is partly about monitoring progress, but also about ensuring you have the support of key stakeholders, so put together a small project board of the power brokers. Arrange the frequency of reporting and meeting so that the team can actually make progress, rather than spending their whole time writing reports and trying to second guess your needs. Once a week is too often, once a quarter is too infrequent. The scale, complexity, and stage of project will determine how often you need to meet.

From a governance perspective you have three simple ways of messing up your project:

● Keep changing your goal and specifications

● Being slow in making decisions

● Once you have made a decision, changing it

Of course, this should not happen. But all three of these are very familiar to anyone who has provided IT projects or been involved in defense procurement. It is a very easy way to ensure cost and time over runs.

THE NATURE OF QUALITY

Which is higher quality: a $100 meal at the Fat Duck or a $2 Big Mac at McDonald's? The answer is, obviously, it depends. It depends on what you mean by quality.

As you eat your snail porridge at the Fat Duck, you will have plenty of time to think about what quality really means. "Quality" has traditionally been associated with high price and exclusivity: handmade Louis Vuitton baggage, tailored suits, and Rolls-Royces. That is a view of quality which is defined by the customer. If a customer believes that high quality bathrooms have gold taps, then gold taps are part of the quality proposition.

For managers, quality is different. Quality is ultimately about consistency, and the absense of defects. If you make a billion microchips, you want a billion microchips that all work in the same way. If you make a billion bottles of cola, you want them all to be the same. **quality is** You do not want one in every million to have a rat's tail in it. **ultimately** And if you make a billion burgers every year, you want the **about** customer to know what they are getting each time will be exactly what they expect: the same as last time. So on this **consistency** metric, McDonald's is better quality than the Fat Duck: it has more consistency and more predictability of taste, offering, and service.

In practice, price affects our perceptions of quality. If we went into McDonald's and they charged us $100 for a Big Mac, we might think it a pretty poor quality offering at that price.

So quality does not exist in a vacuum and is not an end in itself. It is a means to an end: the ultimate end is to make money and grow sustainably. But even the godfather of the modern quality movement, Edward Deming, recognized that quality was simply part of a greater purpose. Deming's first principle of his 14 principles of management was to "become competitive and stay in business, and to provide jobs."

If quality is, for management purposes, mainly about consistency, then that has implications for how it works and where it works. Clearly, consistent quality can and should be achieved wherever there are repetitive tasks to be done: making cars or making burgers can have the full weight of quality practices applied to them. And this is where you will find quality best practiced.

Where jobs are ambiguous and customized, it is much harder to achieve consistent quality. If each job is different, then there can be no consistency. This is the curse of most office and managerial jobs: the jobs are always shifting and consistency is elusive. So the quality movement has not made much progress in the white collar world of law firms, consulting, and other professional services.

But even in the white collar world it is possible to achieve some consistency, and the key is to achieve scale. With scale, jobs can become more specialized and more repetitive. A lone lawyer has to deal with anything and anyone that walks through the door. A large firm can have lawyers specializing in the most arcane aspect of the law. The specialists see the same sorts of case repeatedly, build expertise and can achieve a level of quality which the lone practitioner can never achieve. This is the lesson Adam Smith learned from the pin makers of Gloucester, applied to the modern world: specialization works.

APPLYING QUALITY

Who is the better football player: the fan who buys the replica team shirt and wears it to the stadium, or the professional who is selected for the team and plays in the stadium? Most of us can work out the answer to that one. The fan may look like the professional, but only in his dreams does he play like one.

And yet many managers acted like the sports fan when it came to quality. During the 1980s, Japan appeared to be on the cusp of world domination and quality seemed to be at the heart of its success. So managers went around copying little bits of the Japanese approach to quality: they put in suggestion boxes, or they tried to design better products, or they tried a little bit of *kaizen* (continuous improvement). They bought the replica shirt and showed their allegiance to team quality. But they were never in the same league as the professionals.

Quality is like a heart operation: don't try doing just half of it. Do it all or not at all. Here are some of the principles:

- **Don't inspect for quality at the end;** build quality in from the start (product design) and onward through production.

- **Delegate to the lowest level possible:** let team members monitor their own performance and institute their own improvement ideas.

- **Break down barriers** between departments, suppliers, and customers: everyone has to work together to understand and deliver quality.

- **Get rid of slogans:** slogans do not produce quality, people do.

- **Invest in your team:** constant education and improvement with on-the-job training.

- **Drive out fear** in assessment and rewards, so that people focus on the job and avoid game playing.

Most production and process driven firms that survive have understood that quality is a whole firm effort. And most are applying quality at a more or less competent level: they have to, simply to stay in business. By comparison, most professional services firms with their highly paid partners look like highly inefficient cottage industries. The first person to understand how to drive quality into this world will cause a revolution and make a fortune: they can be the Henry Ford of the 21st century.

RESTRUCTURING THE ORGANIZATION

Every time you reorganize, the old timers will shake their heads knowingly: the corporate carousel keeps on turning and what goes around, comes around. First you have the functional organization, then you move to product focus, then geographic focus, then process focus, then customer focus, then industry focus with all sorts of matrix organizations in between before coming back to the simplicity of the functional organization. They have seen it all before: the more things change, the more they stay the same.

So why bother with all the hassle and grief of reorganization? Occasionally, a well thought through reorganization can genuinely drive efficiency and effectiveness. But even if there is no compelling prospect of the great leap forward in performance, you still have three compelling reasons to reorganize:

- **Take control.** There is nothing like a few ritual executions to concentrate minds. As a new boss, if you reorganize you have the chance to get rid of some power barons and move others around. If you do not deal with the power barons, you may nominally be the ruler but in practice they will be in control. After you have reorganized they will have neither the means nor the will to challenge you.

- **Send a message to your organization** or team about your priorities. Shifting from a product to a customer focus is a simple way of saying, "We have to focus less on our own internal brilliance at designing, making and marketing products and focus more on what our customers really want and how best to serve them." But that means you need to back up your restructuring with changes, where needed, in how you measure and reward people, in your systems, and training. Restructuring is not a standalone activity.

- **Send a message to each member of your team.** Even if you only have a small team, use a restructuring to reset your psychological contract with each member of your team. It is an obvious opportunity. Don't just tell them what their new role is. Take time to explore with them what it really means: how you expect them to behave and perform, how they can benefit, how you can help, and what the change means for them.

Restructuring is not just about structures. It is about people.

REENGINEERING

Over the years reengineering has become cost cutting with a smile. And the smile is optional. So reengineering has a bad name. It conjures up images of highly paid young consultants mapping all your internal processes, turning your organization inside out and then leaving you with a big bill. This is a shame, because reengineering as it was originally created is a very powerful idea. At its heart are three ideas which all managers can use.

1 **Focus on the customer.** Reengineering does not start with your internal procedures and processes. It starts by understanding what the customer wants and what we need to deliver to them. From this simple insight, you can revolutionize your business by stripping out unnecessary services and processes. Eliminating a process is more powerful than streamlining it. Arguably the discount airlines and discount hotels have taken this approach to an extreme: everything that is strictly not necessary for your flight or hotel stay has become an ancillary service for which you usually pay full market rate plus.

2 **Focus on processes not functions.** When IT, operations, marketing, R&D are all doing their own thing, they may do it very well but the result can be that nothing actually gets done for the customer. Success does not come from each function optimizing its own performance. It comes from integrating all the functions to deliver a market result economically. And most of the waste between functions comes about because of management: each functional manager defends territory, so decision making gets slowed down, costs increase, and the competition kick sand in your face.

3 **Simplify your processes.** This is like the parlor game where you have to speak on a given subject for a minute without hesitation, deviation, or repetition. And that is what a good, customer driven process looks like:

   a No hesitation: no down time for slow decision making, waiting for parts or approvals. Delay causes waste.
   b No deviation. The process should be relevant to a market need and should deliver value to the firm. If it does not, cut it.
   c No repetition. Rework is a disaster for costs, time, and quality.

As ever, simplicity triumphs over complexity. The PC industry shows what can be done. In the days before Dell, the PC industry was a classic make and sell business. PC makers made computers and then tried to sell them. So their core process was 1) make and 2) sell. All very sensible. Except that if you forecasted incorrectly, then you were left with excess stock and fire sales, or you missed out on revenues by underselling and would then desperately try to ramp up production and reduce time to market while beating up on your forecasting department. It was, in other words, business as usual.

if you want to do reengineering, be bold

Michael Dell did not have the money to make computers before selling them. So he took a radical step: he sold the computers and then figured out how to make them. It was a classic, if accidental, form of reengineering. His core process was not "make and then sell" but 1) sell and then 2) make. He turned the industry upside down. With that one change, he got rid of all the problems of forecasting, stock outs, fire sales, and reducing time to market. And in the process he made himself a billionaire. So if you want to do reengineering, be bold. Reengineering your HR evaluation system misses the point. To be effective, it has to be a whole firm effort.

USING CONSULTANTS

Everyone loves to hate consultants, and yet everyone uses them. We hate them because they are paid more than us, they have access to the CEO, they are too smart for their own good, and they don't have to endure the hard grind of day-to-day management. And they have an MBA. But we still use them because... why do we use them?

If you find that your consultants cost too much, deliver too little, have taken up squatters' rights in your office, and are a parody of bad consulting, whose fault is that? We get what we deserve, even when it comes to consultants.

For the most part, consultants want to do a good job for you, however surprising that may seem. It is in their interests to do a good job for you, because they really, really want to sell the next piece of work to you. They want a relationship, even if you do not. Their simple rule of thumb is that it costs seven times as much to sell to a new client than it does to an existing client; and existing clients give larger assignments. The career of the smooth partner taking you out to dinner depends on hitting their annual sales target, and you are their best prospect.

Making the most of consultants

1 Make hiring consultants a top level decision and always refuse the first request for help. Make your managers work hard to justify the need for calling in consultants.

2 Be very clear about the brief and the business benefit, and then stick to it. Do not allow scope creep from the consultants: the budget is the budget.

3 Only hire consultants if managers admit they are incapable of doing the job themselves: this should rule out using consultants to justify a decision for which the manager wants support.

4 Once again, insist on the A team: the partner who sells to you will be under pressure to use the untried and untested and to give a second chance to any random consultants within the firm who have not been assigned. The consulting firm will push

back at you having any say over the team, but fight your corner: you would not leave other vital hiring decisions to a blind date process.

5   Give 100% cooperation: be quick to provide documents, make introductions. They are racking up billings very fast, so make the most of every minute. Make sure the whole organization is cooperating, not passively blocking them.

6   Don't waste time putting your staff onto their team for training: any skills that are transferred will not be used, and you will only slow the consultants down. That is very costly to you.

7   Put in place good governance: regular reviews and quick decision making will keep the project on track.

8   Dangle the carrot and then take it away: let the consultants slave for the follow up work which they will identify. And don't give it to them, unless it meets criteria 1–3 above.

DEALING WITH THE LAW

With the law, prevention is always better than cure. So make sure you have a good lawyer. A good lawyer is one who finds how you can do things, not one who finds why you can't do things. And they will help you avert disaster. As a rule, when you go to litigation you have already lost: in many cases it is simply not worth contesting employment cases or customer disputes. The cost exceeds any potential benefit.

Increasingly, business has become a legal minefield. Firms are continually hit by three things:

● Some employees regard the law as a free lottery ticket: win an employment case and make a million. Real or perceived slights and injustices can be turned into big winnings by lawyers keen to take their cut of the employee's hurt.

● Government regulation gives firms ever more opportunity to fall foul of new environment, health, safety, and employment legislation. The intention of the legislation is often good, the application by zealous officials can ruin a firm.

- By the time clients go to law, you will have lost them. So the best defense is to avoid the problem in the first place. There are three classic legal problems with customers (and suppliers):
  - Know when you have a contract. Just because you have not signed a formal contract does not mean you do not have one. If money has been exchanged for actual or expected services, a contract has already arisen. The lawyers will make a fortune finding out what the nature of the contract was based on your email traffic, witness statements and the like.
  - Just because you have a contract does not mean you can enforce it. In dealing with retail customers, the Unfair Contract Terms Act does what it says: you cannot impose unfair terms. For instance, you cannot get a client to sign away all their statutory rights and you cannot exempt yourself from all liability if your product or service fails catastrophically and causes damage.
  - Know when you have liability. Even better, assume you are liable. In common law there is a basic concept of "duty of care" which you owe to employees, customers and others who deal with you. You cannot contractually sign away your duty of care.

Finally, if it all goes wrong and you are sued: don't panic. Do not get emotionally involved, it is a waste of time and effort. Your righteous indignation will have at best no impact, and possibly a very negative impact, on legal proceedings. I was sued for $12 billion. Find the best advice and let the lawyers get on with it. You would not think of personally designing your IT systems, and you should not think of building your legal case. Let the experts do it so that you can focus on your day job.

6

Lead your team

INTRODUCTION

Business schools struggle with leadership. They all have ideas and theories about leadership, but find it very difficult to teach. That is not because business schools are defective, but because leadership cannot be taught in the classroom. MBA courses excel at transferring bodies of explicit knowledge: these are know-what skills like finance and accounting. Business schools cannot teach tacit knowledge or know-how skills like leadership. Know-how skills are typically learned from experience.

The purpose of this chapter is not to transform you into a great leader within 20 pages of brilliant prose. The goal is humbler: to show what challenges leaders normally face inside the firm, and how you can better deal with them. There are consistent patterns of failure and success, and it pays to know what they are in advance.

HOW TO TAKE CONTROL

Just because you have been given a position of power does not mean you are in power. Even at CEO level, there a plenty of people who have the title but they are not leading: they are simply administrators of a legacy that they inherited from the last executive. This is your challenge: make sure you are in control.

Follow four steps to take control:

1 **Have a plan.** A good plan, or a vision if you want to be grand, is a story in four parts which you should be able to communicate in 40 seconds or less.

   a "This is where we are."

   b "This is where we are going (and how it will be different from the past)."

   c "This is how we will get there." This part will be sketchy to start with, and will become clearer and more detailed over time. Do not wait for all the detail to be clear before announcing the overall direction: you will never make any progress. ·

   d "This is your really important and worthwhile role in helping us get there." Make your plan personal to each person you speak to, and be clear about how they can help. This is motivating for your staff and gives clarity to your colleagues.

2 **Get the right support, both within your team and beyond.** The A team will make molehills out of mountains; the B team will make mountains out of molehills. Just because you inherited a team, you do not have to stick with

it. Try to move fast, because no team likes uncertainty. Beyond your team, you need support from key players, including your boss, the technocrats, and colleagues who are important to your plan. Invest time in building that support early, so you do not face constant battles later on.

3   **Get the right budget, both in terms of what you must deliver and in terms of the resources available to you.** As with your team, do not lie down and accept what you have been given, unless it is what you need. The best time to negotiate on budget is before you start in your new role: as soon as you start you will have lost most of your negotiating power, unless you can bring some very compelling new data to the table.

4   **Set expectations fast and set them low.** Your predecessor may have made all sorts of promises on your behalf (all of your team will expect promotion, your bosses will expect sales to triple next year...). If you accept those promises and expectations, you accept failure: you will not measure up to the expected miracles. Find all the skeletons in all the closets and put them on display. Paint a picture of a unit on the verge of imminent collapse. If your view is accepted, then even survival will be seen as success.

All of this means that your first 30 days are critical. You do not have time on your side, especially as most of your colleagues will judge you on first impressions. If you take control successfully, you will be unusual: many managers end up drifting with the tide.

WHAT YOUR TEAM WANTS FROM YOU

There is plenty of advice on how to be a boss, but no one asks the team what they really want from the boss. So I have asked thousands of team members what they expect from a good boss. The results were surprisingly consistent across industries, levels in the firm, and nationality. Here are the top five things your team is likely to expect from you as a boss:

- Vision
- Ability to motivate
- Decisiveness
- Good in a crisis
- Honesty

These are relatively low hurdles over which most bosses trip. You do not have to be great to be a good boss. Here is what each of the five priorities mean:

VISION This is the simple four-part story outlined in the last section—how to take control:

- This is where we are.
- This is where we are going.
- This is how we are going to get there.
- This is your (very important) role in helping us get there.

ABILITY TO MOTIVATE This is where managers fail the most: managers manage upward much better than they manage downward: their boss is more important to their career than their team. Read the section on how to motivate (p. 103).

DECISIVENESS Teams and people hate uncertainty, which leads to doubt and to fear. They also resent the rework and delay that go with indecisiveness. Even when you feel uncertain, project confidence. Always wear the mask of leadership: do not let your uncertainty and doubt spread to your team. If you have to change course, then change course: your team may grumble, but not as much as if you make no decision at all.

always wear the mask of leadership

GOOD IN A CRISIS Crises make or break leaders' reputations. Crises lead to fear, uncertainty, and doubt. Your job is not just to deal with the crisis, but to give others the confidence to follow you. That means you must:

- **Be decisive and positive:** give clear direction and move to action.
- **Project confidence**, even if you have doubt in your heart. Wear the mask.
- **Give support** to those who need it. Avoid the blame game, leave the autopsy until later.
- **Provide air cover:** deal with the politics and noise that surround crises. Let your team get on with the work, rather than worry about the noise.
- **Over-communicate:** recognize that there will be confusion and doubt. Don't let the doubt and the rumors build. Communicate positively, consistently and frequently.

HONESTY This is the most divisive criterion. In the eyes of team members, managers who rated poorly on this rated poorly on everything else. Managers who rated well on honesty had a chance of rating well overall. We found that honesty is not simply the absence of dishonesty. It is stronger than that. Honesty is about trust. No one wants to work with a boss they do not trust. And for team members, trust came down to four simple tests and moments of truth:

- Can I trust my boss to do what they say?

- Can I trust my boss with my promotion and bonus?

- Will my boss be honest, open, and constructive with me about my performance?

- Can I rely on my boss to back me when I get into a corner?

If you can pass the test on those questions, you have a chance of meeting your team's expectations of you.

Finally, note what is absent from your team's expectations of you. They do not expect you to be charismatic and inspirational. This is just as well. Most of the bosses I have had or have interviewed would fail a charisma test. You cannot learn or acquire charisma. But you can acquire the other criteria expected of a good boss. If you meet your team's top five expectations you will set yourself apart from most other bosses, and you will earn their loyalty.

SETTING GOALS

You know that goals should be SMART:

- **S**pecific

- **M**easurable

- **A**ttainable

- **R**elevant

- **T**ime limited

SMART goals are better than the opposite:

- Non-specific: vague

- Not-measurable

- Unachievable

- Irrelevant

- No time limit

SMART goals may be simple, but applying them is not. The real questions about goal setting are:

- What is a reasonable goal?

- Do I know the goal has been accepted and understood?

- Will the goal be achieved or not?

What is a reasonable goal?

The problem with managerial and office work is that it is very ambiguous. You can ask for a report by Wednesday, and you will get a report by Wednesday. It could be either a 200-page report or a two-page report, and it could be brilliant or it could be useless. The goal will have met the SMART criteria but you have no way of knowing in advance whether you will get what you want.

In practice, you have two ways of knowing how much is enough workload for anyone. First, you will probably have direct experience of completing a task similar to the one you are setting, so you should know how much effort it takes. But you do not know how much spare capacity and spare time the person to whom you are delegating has. You may unwittingly be asking a team member to work past midnight for the next two weeks. You know the workload of the goal you are setting, but you do not know the overall workload of each team member in detail.

The simplest way of managing overall workload is to ask. You know who the shirkers are on your team. More problematic are the wannabe heroes who never duck any challenge, however great. So for these people, manage their overall workload by looking out for the pizza boxes. When the office is too full of too many, half eaten, late night pizzas, you have set an unreasonable workload. And if they don't eat pizza, look for the other early warning signs: increased irritability, tiredness, more minor errors creeping into work, and under-communciation. These are all signs of someone wilting under increasing pressure.

Do I know that the goal has been accepted and understood?

As ever, the best way of checking is to ask. Ask your team member to paraphrase back to you what you are asking them to do. People tend to hear what they want to hear. You have to check that they have heard what you said, not what they wanted you to say. And then you can ask them if they agree with what you have asked them to do.

Do I know if the goal will be achieved?

You can set a goal and, by doing so, you delegate away some of your responsibility. But you cannot delegate away your accountability. You are still accountable for the outcome. In President Truman's words: "The buck stops here." So make sure that the goal you set has a reasonable chance of being achieved. Once again, from your own experience, you should know what is achievable in what sort of time frame. But you need to check your own expectations. We all tend to see the past through rose tinted glasses and we forget just how hard and how time consuming it was to complete the sort of tasks we now delegate to others.

The best way of checking yourself is to ask your team member if they think the goal can be achieved in a timely fashion. Ask them what obstacles they see and what help they want. Don't just set the goal and walk away. Your discussion about obstacles and support builds buy-in and commitment.

Of course, you then need to monitor progress and continue to support as required.

HOW TO DELEGATE

Some managers think they delegate well when they delegate all the routine rubbish and, of course, all the blame. This pleases the manager more than the team. Effective delegation is the way to better performance for the boss and the team, but it requires courage, discipline, and self-awareness.

Ten simple tips on good delegation

1 **Know your value.** If you are doing tasks which you did in your previous role, you should not have been promoted. Demote yourself. You do not add value by doing the job of your team, even if you think you can do it better than they can. You must do something different from the team: organize and build the team; manage the politics; find the right assignments.

2   **If in doubt, delegate.** There is very little that cannot be delegated. Ricardo Semler has built one of the biggest businesses in Brazil (Semco SA) by delegating everything: teams even decide on their own pay and conditions and hire their managers.

3   **Be clear about outcomes:** what you expect and when you expect it. Even if you have to brief the team three times to achieve clarity, do so. If there is any room for ambiguity, you will be misunderstood. Do not blame the team, blame yourself: your team is not psychic and cannot read your mind. Clarity avoids rework, conflict, and loss of morale and confidence later on.

4   **Be flexible about the means.** You may think you are the only person who knows how to do anything properly. But let your team surprise you: they may even come up with a better way of doing the task.

5   **Let go.** Do not check every five minutes to see how the team is performing. Show some trust in your team, and if they are any good they will respond by making it happen. You will need regular updates, but if you have too many of them the team will spend all their time preparing updates for you, not doing the actual work.

6   **Be available.** Encourage the team to talk through any issues they have. Do not dictate the answer to them: help them discover the answer themselves. You do not need to show your brilliance by telling them the answer: they will simply learn to depend on you for everything.

7   **Stretch the team.** Pressure is good: that is how people find a sense of accomplishment, find new and creative ways of doing things and develop new skills. But if pressure is good, stress is bad. The difference is control: as long as they feel under control they will experience pressure, not stress. Delegating well gives them control and avoids stress. You will know when you have overstretched them: they will complain.

8   **Delegate meaningful work**, not just the routine tasks. Do not keep all the juicy jobs for yourself.

9   **Never delegate the blame**, unless you want a dysfunctional and political team. You can delegate authority, you cannot delegate responsibility: you are always responsible for the outcomes of your team.

10 **Delegate the praise.** This strengthens you: it builds loyalty, trust, and respect from your team. It also shows your bosses and colleagues that you are a smart and effective boss. By delegating praise you attract praise yourself.

HOW TO MOTIVATE: THE THEORY

At some point in your managerial life, you will learn about Maslow's hierarchy of needs. It will be presented as the answer to the conundrum of what motivates people. So here is a short guide to the original theory, and a more practical alternative that you can use day to day.

Maslow rightly observed that we are all needs junkies. We all need something: and once we have achieved that initial something, we move on to wanting something more. The wanting never goes away: the object of our desire simply changes. The only known cure is to retreat to a Buddhist monastery and learn the art of detachment through meditation: it works, but may not be good for your career ambitions.

Below are Maslow's hierarchy of needs as he presented them: the italics show what those needs look like in the workplace.

1 **Physiological:** food, water. *Having a job, any job.*

2 **Safety:** shelter, protection. *Job security, pay, and conditions.*

3 **Love:** family and friends. *Belonging to a worthwhile team and goal.*

4 **Esteem:** recognized by your peers. *Recognition and success.*

5 **Self-actualization:** achieving meaning and purpose in life. *Leaving a legacy.*

If you have no job, no income and a large mortgage, any job can look attractive. But as that need is filled, you are likely to aspire to higher things. By the time you become a CEO, you may be aiming for the huge pay-off and a knighthood/damehood before retiring: there is always something more that people want. So up to a point, Maslow works.

In practice, it is hard to know where people are in Maslow's hierarchy of needs. Asking a colleague if they are in need of love could be misinterpreted. And it is not always clear what in practice you can do about it. So we need something simpler.

In practice, people are motivated by four things:

● Greed

● Fear

● Sex

● Idleness

We will ignore sex, although that has been used as a career weapon with great effect down the ages. You make your own choice on that. That leaves us with greed, fear, and idleness.

GREED This is simple. As Maslow showed, there is always something more which everyone wants. Take time to find out what it is. The simple act of finding out and respecting other people's interests goes far in building trust. But

don't give in to greed: use it

remember, the more you give, the more they want. As soon as the bonus is paid, they want a promotion. As soon as the promotion is in the bag, they want the foreign post. Don't give in to greed: use it. Make people work hard for their dream. Dangle the carrot in front of them, but do not let them eat it. Keep them hungry.

FEAR Maslow's hierarchy of needs works in reverse: there is always something we fear. We do not want to go backward. If we have recognition, we do not want to lose it. If we have a strong sense of belonging, we do not want to lose that—and we certainly do not want to lose our jobs. Threatening people with loss instils compliance, but not commitment. Show that you can help someone avoid their worst fears (and that their worst fears have a real chance of coming true), and you will find you have a willing ally.

IDLENESS Plenty of people want to become a top movie star, singer, athlete, professor, or even politician. But that takes both effort and risk, and there are other things I want to do this evening. So idleness is the drag on our greed, our ambition. Leaders and sales people use this to good effect. Make it easy for people to follow and to buy. Make it easy for colleagues to agree with you, and make it awkward and painful for them to disagree. Most will take the easy route.

All of this is the theory. Day to day, you need some simple motivational tools to use. This is the purpose of the next section.

HOW TO MOTIVATE IN PRACTICE

You do not need psychology to work out how to motivate people. Start by thinking about the best boss you ever worked for. What did the boss do to motivate you so well? Do you do the same things with your team?

In reality, we all respond to simple motivational measures. Having asked thousands of people about their jobs, there is one question that consistently indicates how positive or negative you are likely to feel about your work: "my boss cares about me and my career" (agree/disagree). People who have bosses who don't care feel bad about their job and their boss. People who have bosses who care are much more positive.

Caring is not about currying favor and trying to be liked. Caring means having the courage to be honest, to have the difficult conversation about performance in a positive way. You do not need to be liked: you need to be respected.

Ultimately, there is no short cut to motivating people. If you care, you have to invest time in your team. It is investing, not spending or wasting, time. And it is not "quality" time: "quality" is a euphemism for "minimal."

Showing you care is simple to say but hard to do. So how do you show you care? Here are 10 things you can do every day to motivate your team better:

Ten ways to motivate your team

1 **Take time to listen to your team.** Understand their hopes, fears, and dreams. Casual time by the water cooler, rather than a formal expectations meeting in an office, is often the best way to get to know your colleagues and team members.

2 **Say thank you.** We all crave recognition. We want to know we are doing something worthwhile and that we are doing it well. Make your praise real, for real achievement. And make it specific. Avoid the synthetic one-minute manager style praise: "gee, you photocopied that sheet of paper really well...."

3 **Never demean a colleague.** If you have criticism, keep it private and make it constructive. Don't scold them like school children. Treat them as partners and work together to find a way forward.

4 **Delegate well.** Delegate meaningful work which will stretch and develop your team member. Yes, routine rubbish has to be delegated, but delegate some of the interesting stuff as well. Be clear and consistent about your expectations.

5 **Have a vision.** Show where your team is going and how each team member can help you all get there. Have a clear vision for each team member: know where they are going and how you can help them get there.

6 **Trust your team.** Do not micromanage them. Practise MBWA: the gurus call it "manage by walking around." The better version is called "manage by walking away."

7 **Be honest.** Be ready to have difficult but constructive conversations with struggling team members early. Don't shade or hide the truth. Honesty builds trust and respect, provided you are constructive with it.

8 **Set clear expectations.** Be very clear about promotion and bonus prospects, and about the required outcome from each piece of work. Assume that you will be

➡

misunderstood: people hear what they want to hear. So make it simple, repeat it often and be 100% consistent.

9   **Over-communicate.** You have two ears and one mouth: use them in that proportion. Listen twice as much as you speak. Then you will find out what really drives your team members and you can act accordingly.

10 **Don't try to be friends.** It is more important to be respected than it is to be liked. Trust endures where popularity is fickle and leads to weak compromises. If your team trusts and respects you, they will want to work for you.

As with all things that sound simple, in practice it is very hard to do all these things well and to do them consistently. It is high effort, but normally very high reward. Of course, there will always be the occasional member of the awkward squad, but most people will respond well if you show you care.

STYLES COACHING: COACHING, COUNSELING, OR DICTATING?

Coaching is a core management skill which few managers master. If you cannot coach your team, then you end up having to deal with every problem yourself. All the monkeys land on your back, which will frustrate you and it will frustrate your team because you are not giving them the chance to develop and grow. In this sense, coaching goes hand in hand with delegation. Coaching support lets your team learn and helps them take some of the monkeys away.

Coaching has been given a bad name by the coaching industry. Too many coaches turn out to be former executives who have gone into semi-retirement. What they lack in skill, they make up for with process. They learn to answer every question with a question: this avoids the need for them to have any insight of their own. You do their work for them, and then you pay them. This sort of coaching is closer to counseling and therapy: it has its place, which is not in the workplace.

you add value by adding insight

Your team does not need you to be a counselor and therapist. They need you to be a coach. You add value by adding insight, not just by asking questions. And you should be able to add insight, because of your experience. This does not mean you tell your team what to do. You let them discover the best solution. And in the process of letting them work out the best solution, you may well find that they come up with a better solution than the one you had in your mind. More importantly, it will be a solution to which your team member is committed: it is their solution, they own it and they will want it to succeed. If it is your solution, it becomes another half-baked solution from their half-baked boss.

So a good manager-coach steers a very careful line between two traps. Avoid becoming counselor and therapist to the team. Avoid being the benign dictator who solves every problem and gives every direction.

It is always quicker for you in the short term to offer the solution and move on. In the long term, this simply makes the team ever more dependent on you and increases your workload and stress. In the short term, coaching takes time and effort. Think of it as investment in your team. The more they learn to deal with challenges themselves, the easier your life becomes and the better their performance becomes.

The coach-manager supports the team and helps them discover the best solution through a combination of asking questions, adding insight, and sharing experience. How you achieve this goal is the purpose of the next section.

COACHING FOR MANAGERS

Here is a simple framework for coaching a team member when they need help. Think of the five Os:

- **O**bjectives
- **O**utline the situation and explore other perspectives
- **O**ptions
- **O**bstacles to success and offer of help
- **O**utcome and next steps

Here is how each of the Os works in practice.

Objectives

Your team member will have one objective: to find a solution to a problem. But you should have three objectives:

- Help the team member find a solution
- Ensure that the team member owns the solution and is committed to making it happen
- Help the team member develop their own capabilities

The first two objectives are reasonably self-explanatory. The third needs some explaining. Each of your team members will have development needs, which will probably be of a long-term nature. So use your conversation to help them see how they can solve the problem and develop the skill they require at the same time. That should become clear as you work through the rest of the conversation.

Outline the situation and explore other perspectives

Once you have agreed what the problem is that you are trying to solve, ask the team member to outline the situation as they see it. Standard operating procedure is that the person being coached will see themselves as diligent, hard working, and honest while everyone else is idle, incompetent, and untrustworthy. This is not the time to challenge their personal world view directly. But once they have stated their case, ask how other people might see the situation. Explore it from several angles.

As this part of the conversation unfolds, three things should happen.

- First, you should be forming your hypothesis about what the possible set of solutions might be. You can test your ideas by asking directed questions: if you think funding is the issue, ask questions around that.

- Second, the team member will start to see things differently. They may start to see that they are part of the problem (even though they will never say that) and hopefully they will see that they are responsible for the solution: they will stop blaming everything on other people.

- Third, your team member may already be starting to discover potential solutions. The simple act of having the conversation and forcing their thought processes often works wonders.

Do not rush this stage of the conversation. If you rush into exploring options based on partial and garbled information, you are likely to have a train crash. Only when you have a full picture of the challenge, and you have some hypotheses about what to do about it, then you can proceed to the next stage.

Options

Ask your team member how they might address the challenge. Encourage them to think of more than one option. If they offer a single-point solution you have a very limited conversation which may become confrontational if they have not identified a workable solution.

If they have not suggested any solutions you can suggest some options yourself. Your experience should tell you how such challenges have been handled well or poorly on the past. Use that experience to open up a range of options: do not close down options yet.

Once you have identified possible solutions ask the team member to evaluate them: what are the benefits and concerns of each solution? In practice, this part of the conversation rapidly focuses on just two contrasting options. Relevant questions now will ensure that the team member does not fall in love with a catastrophic plan of action.

By now, even the slowest team member should be nudging themselves toward the best solution. The brightest team members will probably be exploring solutions that are better than the ones you had in mind.

Let the team member focus on the solution that they feel most confident about. It is critical that it is their solution, not yours.

Obstacles to success and offer of help

You now need to turn the conversation to action: how is this going to happen and what might stop it happening? You will probably find that an enthusiastic team member can be naive about how easy it will be to turn their idea into action. That is why you have to make them think explicitly about what and who will be a barrier to success. As they identify each barrier, coach them again to think through what it will take to overcome the barrier.

By the time you and the team member are convinced you have a viable way forward, you have nearly won. The next step is to ask if there is anything you can do to help: you should be there to support if necessary, but not to lead. Let them ask for help rather than imposing it. Imposed help is an imposition, does not help, and is rarely valued. Only help if they want it.

Outcomes

This final step is about summarizing and clarifying what you have agreed and what you are going to do. The potential for miscommunication and misunderstanding is huge: both you and the team member have probably heard and remembered what you want to hear and remember. You may well have chosen to remember different things.

You should not summarize: let the team member summarize. When they say it, they commit to it. And you can check their script against yours. If they are different, resolve the difference immediately and avoid tears later on.

GIVING PRAISE

Managers are taught how to give feedback, which is invariably management-speak for criticism. The only thing worse than feedback is constructive feedback: that is when you know you are in serious trouble.

Managers are never taught the even more important art of giving praise. To some managers, praise is for wimps. And yet as individuals, we all crave recognition. If we want recognition for ourselves, we should be prepared to give recognition to other people. Done well, praise is an easy way of building support, respect, and alliances. It is easier to succeed when you have people who actively support you than when you are met with a wall of passive indifference. So praise is not about being nice for the sake of it. Praise is a way of becoming a better manager.

praise is an easy way of building support, respect, and alliances

Here is how to praise well:

- **Be brave.** Find the courage and time to say thank you. You are not being weak by saying thank you.

- **Praise real contributions.** It is a sensible courtesy to thank colleagues for making a photocopy, fixing the coffee, finding a document. A "thank you" does no harm. But if you start lavishing praise on someone for the outstanding way they poured the milk into your coffee, then do not be surprised if you earn a reputation for insincerity: no one will believe you even when your praise is real.

- **Be specific.** Don't thank someone for being a great person, instead thank them for a specific thing they did which helped you. Show why you are grateful: "you're doing a great job" is meaningless; "you saved that client relationship by getting that shipment out on time last night" means something.

- **Make it personal.** Show how their effort helped you; you might even recognize that they went out of their way, or they were doing a thankless task, or that it was unusually difficult.

- **Where appropriate, offer recognition in public.** There is little point in being recognized if no one knows you have been recognized.

Here is how to mess up praise:

- **Focus all your praise on a few favorites.** Exclude and annoy everyone else.

- **Praise trivial things.** Avoid the one-minute manager "well done, you have clean shoes this morning…." At best it is patronizing and it also devalues all your other praise.

- **Be insincere.** If you name-check 50 people in a speech, it will be completely meaningless. If you are specific about what each of 12 people contributed, it means something.

Praise can be subtle and effective. In meetings, you can use praise to get your own way, as follows. Listen to all the arguments around the table. At the right moment, quietly summarize, thanking each person for the wonderful/original/ brilliant insight they brought to the table. Watch as each person around the table puffs up with pride at having their brilliance recognized. Naturally, you will focus only on the points that support your position. By the time you finish your summary, everyone will be rooting for you because they think you are supporting what they have said. At a milder level, simply build on someone else's idea: "Dan made a great point there, and it made me think (enter your point of view here)." That simple public praise starts to bring Dan around to your side: he now sees you as an ally.

One of the best managers I know makes a habit of ensuring he praises at least 10 times as often as he criticises. He keeps score. His criticisms are sufficiently unusual that people sit up and take notice. He has now found that even his occasional criticisms are a mistake. He can normally achieve the same outcome by making a positive and supportive suggestion which leads to action. He is one of those rare bosses that people want to work for, rather than having to work for.

HOW TO CRITICIZE

Criticism is kryptonite in any organization. Most of us have thin skins. We like to believe we are not defective models when it comes to being human. As a test, rate yourself as below or above average on the following:

- Honesty
- Kindness
- Hard work
- Ability to drive a car
- Parenting skills
- Competence at work

About 95% of humans rank themselves in the top 50% of humanity on most criteria. This is statistically impossible but emotionally inevitable. It is normal not to see ourselves as defective, but as a manager your criticism will suggest that your staff are defective in some way. It should be no surprise when our well meaning advice (criticism as the other person sees it) can become a case of "light fuse and stand well back." The result is either an explosion or a long sulk.

So the first rule of criticism is do not criticize or offer unwanted advice, unless the criticism will help the individual or organization succeed better. If someone has bad hair, bad teeth, bad dress, bad jokes, bad car and has an unfashionable pastime, that is their problem, not yours. Unless of course these defects affect their prospects or the prospects of your business.

If you are to criticize, make sure you have the right context and the right process. The right context means:

- **The right time.** If you offer criticism while a colleague is still bouncing off the walls with frustration at a setback this simply adds fuel to the fire. Equally, if you leave it months before raising the issue, you have missed your chance. Deal with the issue as soon as possible, when your colleague is in a calm and receptive mood.

- **The place.** Criticism and advice should always be in private. Public criticism is ritual humiliation which leads first to loss of face and then to loss of employee, followed possibly by a lawsuit.

- **The right goal.** The intention is not to show someone is a failure: that sets up conflict. The goal is to find a better way of doing things. So the style should be collaborative, positive, and action focused. It should not be an analysis of past failings: that leads to arguments, not to progress or improvement. Before you start you need to be clear in your mind about what the desired outcome should be.

The right process can be summarized with a simple acronym: SPIN.

- **S: situation.** This is a simple review of the facts: "I noticed that you were late in to work for four client meetings last week." Agree the facts: if you are wrong, apologize and move on. If the other person goes into denial, then probably you have picked the wrong time for the discussion. Find a time when you will be dealing with reason, not emotion.

- **P: personal impact** or "this is how it made me feel." For instance: "Being late makes me think you do not care about client work...." Again, it is hard to argue with feelings. And it offers the chance for the other person to state their position.

- **I: Inquire.** This is about asking questions to find a constructive way forward. You should be listening 85% of the time, rather than giving your grand view on how someone else can be less defective. First, enquire about why this problem is occurring. It may be because of a problem you had not been aware of. Then, ask how they would like to change things: they have to suggest the solution. They will only act if it is their plan, not yours. So take your time, let them work it out for themselves, with your help.

- **N: Next steps.** This is where you get them to summarize. Be specific about what will happen when. And ask if there is any support they need or you can give: make sure they cannot come back with more excuses later on.

By the end of the conversation, they should feel that they have found a positive way forward and that you have supported them on that journey. They should not feel that they have been scolded like a school child and told to do something they do not want to do.

MANAGING MBAs AND OTHER PROFESSIONALS

The most unrealistic thing about TV soap operas is that the characters never mention the soap opera in conversation. The most surprising omission from an MBA is that it does not teach you how to manage MBA types. Managing MBAs is different from managing other colleagues; the more prestigious the MBA, the more distinctive the challenge becomes.

managing MBAs is different from managing other colleagues

Top MBA graduates can be very high maintenance but very high performance. The trick is to maximize the performance and minimize the maintenance. If there is such a thing as a typical top MBA graduate then he or she will:

- Have very high expectations and ambition

- Have a big but fragile ego

- Be a natural over-achiever

- Be naive about handling people, at least early on in their career

So how do you handle such a person?

- **Stretch them.** They are natural over-achievers, so let them over-achieve. Set stretching goals and timings and they will work all hours to over-deliver. If they are not stretched they become like the very bright kid at school who is bored by the lessons and becomes disruptive before going into a self-defeating vortex of doom.

- **Give them autonomy.** They will resist being micromanaged because it is against their dignity and they probably do not have great respect for you or any of their bosses. They think they are smarter and better than anyone else, including you.

- **Never demean them.** They find it hard to take criticism, even in private. So keep your difficult conversations positive: focus on what needs to happen next and drive them forward that way.

- **Set clear expectations and boundaries.** They will want it all and want it now: be clear about bonus and promotion expectations and stay very firm and very consistent.

- **Make them feel they are doing an important and worthwhile job.** Even mundane work can be sold as important: if they have to read 5,000 pages of routine documentation for an M&A deal, then clearly the success or failure of the deal may rely on them picking up a problem in the paperwork. Dull work, worth billions.

- **Be their pooper scooper in chief.** They will mess up dealing with other people and you will need to clear up. They will always believe that it is the fault of the other person who is not so smart, hard working, etc. Coach them in private to help them understand that it does not matter whose fault it is: they have to get the result. Slowly, they will learn to adapt their style to those of other people so that they can get their way.

All of these rules apply to managing all professionals and perhaps all staff. The risks and rewards associated with MBAs simply raise the stakes.

Dealing with colleagues

INTRODUCTION

When I coach executives, I very rarely find that any of their challenges are to do with tasks or techniques. Nearly all the challenges which executives find most challenging are other people: colleagues, team members, and bosses. Unfortunately, people cannot be managed like accounts: you cannot insist they conform to standard rules and that they should all balance at the end of the month. For better or worse, people have minds of their own. As managers, we have to deal with them to get results.

Dealing with people is getting harder all the time. The days of command and control are long gone. If we are to succeed, we have to make things happen through people who we do not control. We have to learn the subtle arts of persuasion, influence, and occasional hard ball. Because there is no rule book for dealing with people, this is the skill which most managers struggle hardest with. We learn mainly from experience of messing up and occasionally succeeding, or by watching others mess up and succeed. This is a long, slow random walk of experience. Most of us do not have the time or patience for this slow walk.

Although there is no rule book, there are some fairly predictable principles of success and failure. If we can learn the principles, then we can decide how to apply them in practice and in the style which best suits each one of us.

COLLEAGUES OR COMPETITORS?

Who is your deadliest competitor? The people you really need to fear are those who can take away your promotion, seize your bonus pool, get their priorities put ahead of yours when it comes to management time and support, and can mess up your projects and proposals. So your real competition is not in the marketplace. Your real competition is sitting at a desk near you. Your colleagues are your deadliest competitors, but also your most important collaborators in making things happen.

your real competition is sitting at a desk near you

To make your task more interesting, your firm probably extols the virtues of team work. So you have to work with people with whom you are competing, and all of them think that they are at the center of the universe, have the most important and urgent tasks, and that they are the good people surrounded by mendacious, idle, and incompetent colleagues.

Succeeding in such a contradictory, and possibly dysfunctional, environment requires a certain mindset. You need a simple set of rules to guide you in dealing with your colleagues and the organization. Each firm and each individual has their own unique success formula. You need to build yours and make it fit with your firm. But in practice there are some fairly universal rules that can be adapted to most firms.

The universal rules

- **Focus on the mission of the firm.** At one level this is about doing what is right for the greater good of the firm. But it also means understanding the agenda of top management and making sure that what you do is aligned with their needs. This gives you power and relevance when fighting your corner.

- **Collaborate and be seen to collaborate.** You can only get things done through other people you do not control. You need allies across the organization. If you pick unnecessary fights then even if you win the fight, you earn yourself an enemy.

- **Build trust.** You do not need to like or be liked by colleagues: management is not a popularity contest. And even if you are liked, popularity is fickle; trust is a more enduring and valuable currency. You can build trust by showing that you understand and respect colleagues' needs and agenda and by being 100% reliable: you must always deliver on promises, however great or small.

- **Protect your interests.** Most fights are pointless, some are necessary. You have to make sure you get the right assignments, right team, and right budget. If these are wrong, you have a recipe for misery.

- **Build support.** Make sure you have a sponsor at least two levels above you. You do not want to be a slave to your immediate boss, who may or may not be good. And you need a senior person who can help you fix political logjams, watch your back and identify emerging career opportunities. So make yourself useful to senior colleagues in whatever way you can.

- **Be flexible.** Your colleagues are different. They have different styles of dress, thinking and acting; they have different needs and expectations. You have your ways. No one is right or wrong, even though you will believe in the righteousness of your position. See the world through the warped eyes of your colleagues and adapt your approach accordingly. The shortest route between two points may be a straight line, but when you are sailing against the wind the quickest route is a zigzag. Learn to zigzag through your firm.

UNDERSTANDING YOURSELF

You cannot understand yourself until you understand how you affect other people. Other people are different from you. Even more importantly, you appear different from your colleagues. They may not intuitively recognize that you are wonderful, intelligent, diligent and great with people.

There are plenty of psychological self-assessment tools to use on the Web. One of the most popular profiling tools remains MBTI (Myers Briggs Type Indicators). MBTI may not be the best or most reliable diagnostic, but it is the most widely used. So it makes sense to understand it. You don't need to go through the formal accreditation process as this can take years, which totally misses the point. The point is not to become an expert at MBTI: the point is to have a quick way of working out how people are different and what you can do about it.

Here is MBTI as you may see it in the first three columns. You will never see the negative impact column because MBTI trainers are fearful of offending anyone. In practice, the negative column is often the easiest way to spot your style, and to recognize how it may be limiting your progress.

Type	Description	Positive impact	Negative impact
Extroversion (E)	Gains energy from others. Speaks, then thinks.	Spreads energy and enthusiasm.	Loudmouth; does not include other people.
Introversion (I)	Gains energy from within. Thinks before speaking.	Thoughtful. Gives space to others.	Nothing worth saying? Uneasy networker.
Sensing (S)	Observes outside world. More facts, less ideas.	Practical, concrete and detailed.	Dull. Unimaginative.
Intuitive (N)	Pays attention to inner world, self, and ideas.	Creative and imaginative.	Flighty and impractical.
Thinking (T)	Decides with head and logic.	Logical, rational, and intellectual.	Cold and heartless.
Feeling (F)	Listens to the heart.	Empathetic, understanding.	Soft headed. Fuzzy thinker, bleeding heart.
Judging (J)	Organized, scheduled, tidy.	High work ethic, focused and reliable.	Compulsive neat freak, uptight, rigid, and rule bound.
Perceiving (P)	Keeps options open, opportunistic.	Work–life balance, enjoys work.	Lazy, messy, and unreliable.

As you look at the positive list, it is only human nature to think that you have all the positive qualities listed. That is not how MBTI works. You have to choose between:

- E and I
- S and N
- T and F
- J and P

The result is an acronym to describe you such as ENTP or ISTJ. It is a way of categorizing people and of putting people in boxes. But people should not be put in boxes until they are dead. And it is far too hard to work out which boxes to put someone in, let alone do anything about it, in day-to-day life. So the real use of MBTI is to get a measure of yourself and understand how you affect other people. Make the most of your positive impacts, but be aware that every positive has a negative. If someone reacts badly to you, the MBTI framework may help you identify a possible style clash which you have with that person. You then have the knowledge to do something about it, if you wish.

UNDERSTANDING OTHERS

In practice, you need a faster shorthand to understand other people. That is the purpose of this section. Churchill described Russia as "a riddle, wrapped in a mystery, inside an enigma." People are even harder to understand. But Churchill helped solve his own Russian riddle: "Perhaps there is a key. That key is Russian national interest." And so it is with people: the key is self-interest. That is the starting point for understanding others. Look at the world through their eyes, understand their needs, hopes, and fears and you have a chance of influencing them well.

However, you need to go even further. Understand their character: how they like to work and what they dislike. If you can understand their style, you are well placed to work with them.

Here is a list of character traits you can probably find around you:

- Risk taking versus risk averse
- Sensitive versus thick skinned
- Quick versus slow
- Decisive versus indecisive

- Afternoon person versus morning person
- Prompt versus tardy
- Controlling versus empowering
- Receptive versus assertive
- Cooperative versus competitive
- Altruistic versus materialistic
- Honest versus devious
- People focused versus task focused
- Inductive versus deductive thinking
- Big picture versus detailed thinker
- Practical versus imaginative
- Progressive versus traditional
- Talker versus thinker
- Words versus numbers
- Analytical versus action focused

You can create an endless list of trade-offs. The point is that everyone is different, so treat them differently. Do not try to make an analytical, risk averse, and practical person into an action focused, risk-taking ideas person. It will end in tears. Work to the strengths of the other person, be it your team member, colleague, or boss. If your boss is best in the late afternoon, don't set meetings for 8am when he or she is Mr. or Mrs. Grumpy. Even if you are a morning person, if you want the best out of the other person, work to their style.

work to the strengths of the other person

Try this simple exercise. Make a list of the four trade-offs that best define the person you need to influence (either from the list above, or from those which mean most in your context). Focus on their character, not yours. Then see where you are on the same trade-offs. If you share the same characteristics, you may find you get along well naturally. If you are at opposite ends you have ample room for misunderstanding. Your job is to adapt so that the other person feels comfortable dealing with you.

NEGOTIATING JUDO: SUCCEED WITHOUT FIGHTING

Negotiating is not just for negotiators. All managers have to negotiate with colleagues, bosses, team members, and others to get their way. It can take years to become an expert negotiator. But here are seven tips to turn negotiating warfare into negotiating judo: succeed without fighting.

Seven tips for successful negotiating

1 **Listen.** Good negotiators have two ears and one mouth: do you qualify? If so, use them in that proportion: listen twice as much as you talk. The more they talk, the more you find out about how to pitch your idea, and the more likely they are to talk themselves into submission.

2 **Ask open questions to encourage more talking.** Open questions are ones to which it is not possible to answer yes or no. How, what, why type questions get rich answers.

3 **Paraphrase.** Don't argue with the other party. Simply sum up what they have said, and perhaps even show you share the same concerns. By summarizing, you show you have understood and you open up the way to finding points of agreement, not disagreement.

4 **Contradict.** Contradict the other person to gain agreement??? Yes. Offer them the chance to show off how clever they are and put you in your place. For instance, you have a really awkward job that needs doing. Approach the plumber, printer, IT person and say, "I don't think you can do this, that's what others have said, but I thought I ought to tell you about it . . ." See the other side bristle with indignation: they will tell you that of course they can do it. They talk themselves into doing the awkward job.

5 **Let them talk about themselves.** If in doubt, get the other side to talk about their favorite subject: themselves. Coo over their trivial triumphs and nod sagely over their immense challenges. The more they talk, the more they will think you are a wonderful person for understanding them so well. The business discussion becomes easy.

6 **Summarize.** In a room of six people you may hear seven different views. Watch and listen as the blood is spilled. When everyone has fought themselves into a stalemate,

➡

quietly offer (as a neutral) to summarize discussion. Pick up on at least one excellent and insightful comment each person has made. Watch them agree because they have had their genius idea recognized in public. They will agree with your summary because no one argues with their own idea. Of course, your summary will be selective and will just happen to reinforce the view you started the meeting with. Done well, everyone meekly falls into line and goes on to the next agenda item.

7 **Focus on the win–win:** find the areas of agreement. Get behind the stated position (I want a lower upfront price) to find the real interest (lowest lifetime costs, cost in use) which may lead to a completely different position (pay more up front to minimize total costs).

Of course, knowing how and when to deploy each tactic takes time to learn. But perhaps the most important lesson of all is easy to learn: negotiate. Most people lose because they do not even try to negotiate. If you don't ask, you don't get ....

HOW TO DISAGREE AGREEABLY (HOW TO TURN DISAGREEMENT INTO AGREEMENT)

Never argue with toddlers, taxi drivers, or God: even if you are right, it will do you no good. And arguing with colleagues or bosses is nearly as bad: you either lose the argument or you lose an ally. But you need a way of dealing with their latest hair-brained idea without losing face, or losing your job.

So how do you disagree, get your way, and avoid turning a colleague into a lifelong enemy? Your goal is to achieve a win–win, not a win–lose outcome. Think judo, not boxing: use your colleague's momentum to your advantage.

Here's how, in five (not so easy) steps:

1 **Listen.** Don't argue, disagree, or interrupt. Encourage them to complete their explanation of their idea. They want to be heard and respected. If you argue too soon you will be met with "You don't understand... let me explain" and you are into a win–lose time wasting argument.

2 **The nice save.** Start by praising the one element of the idea which is good. Do you tell a new mother that their baby is the ugliest the world has ever seen? A colleague's idea is their baby: don't insult it. Get the colleague emotionally on board by finding common ground, however trivial.

3 **Find a common cause.** Go into praise overdrive. Thank your colleague for having the sense/courage/insight to tackle whatever issue they are trying to tackle. Show why the issue is so important: start to focus discussion on the desired outcome, not on the detail of their idea.

4 **Empathize.** Indicate that you had been thinking about the same thing, but struggling with it. You could find no way around three big problems (which just happen to be the three fatal flaws with the idea your colleague has suggested).

5 **Work together to solve 'your' problem.** By now you should have refocused discussion away from their idea (which they will not want to change) to your problem (which they will be keen to show they can solve). The new solution should now provide a very agreeable alternative to the idea which you first encountered. You have won the argument and won a friend. Job done.

Avoid getting caught in the internal logic of their idea or avoid getting dragged into the detail of their suggestion. Quietly shift the discussion away from their scheme. Focus on the end benefits you and they want to achieve and make them think that they are helping and coaching you, rather than you criticizing them.

Once you establish a reputation for tact, even a whisper of disquiet from you will sound like thunder. You build power, credibility, and allies by disagreeing well.

HOW TO HANDLE EXPLODING HEAD SYNDROME

Dealing with Mr. and Mrs. Nasty

Mr. and Mrs. Nasty can be your boss, your customer, or your colleague. You may not want to deal with them, but you have to deal with them. The question is how, especially when tempers and the temperature start to rise and it is hard to stay cool.

There are two sure-fire ways of making things worse:

● **Argue the righteous logic of your position.** Fighting emotion with logic is like fighting fire with fuel: spectacular, but not advisable

● **Get emotional.** As soon as you descend into the sewer with Mr. Nasty, he will get on his high horse and trumpet how unreasonable you are. He wins, you lose.

So if neither logic nor emotion works, what does? The goal is simple to state but hard to achieve. You need to do the following:

- **Stay positive and professional.** How you behave is as important as what you say. Look the part, don't look the fool.

- **Focus on the desired outcome.** Where do you want to be at the end of the conversation? Work toward that end and avoid getting dragged into the mire. As a rule, it is better to win a friend than to win an argument.

- **Focus on common interests, not on narrow positions.** At its simplest a position may be "you messed up"; the common interest is "we need to find a solution."

So how do you stay positive when Mr. and Mrs. Nasty are doing their best to enrage you? I have asked many executives this question, and here are some of the best answers I have heard:

- Imagine what your favorite role model would do in this situation, and then do the same thing. But if your role model is a mix of Darth Vader and Vlad the Impaler, do not use this technique.

- Become a fly on the wall and watch the event. As you detach you will be able to think more clearly and objectively, without getting emotionally involved.

- Imagine Mr. Nasty in a pink tutu. It is hard to get angry with a fat 50-year-old in a pink tutu. Not laughing (or being sick) may be a greater challenge than staying calm.

- Pull out your imaginary Uzi and splatter their brains over the wall. As Mr. Nasty does not even know what you have done, he cannot retaliate.

- Count to 10. Let the immediate flush of anger pass and regain control of your feelings.

- Breathe deeply, as taught in yoga or Buddhist meditation lessons. Like counting to 10, this allows you to regain control and lets you respond professionally.

happiness is the greatest revenge

Finally, remember that happiness is the greatest revenge. Mr. and Mrs. Nasty are nasty today and probably have nasty lives. That is their problem. They may make you stressed today, but tomorrow you will be happy and they will not. You have won.

WHEN TO FIGHT

Conflict is not just inevitable inside organizations: it is good, within reason. Every department, function, and geography has a different window on reality. They see things differently and have different priorities. In theory, they should all pull together behind the grand corporate vision. Meanwhile, back on planet Earth, these different perspectives and priorities lead to competition for those things which count for most, to most managers: budget, bonuses, promotions, and support of top management.

The competing priorities of different groups have to be sorted out. There is always more demand for budget, bonus, and promotion than there is available supply. Internal competition is a healthy way of finding out where best to allocate scarce resources. Less healthily, it also leads to politicking, back stabbing, and ego clashes between power barons.

If you accept that conflict is inevitable, then the big question is when to fight and when to fold. If you never fight, you become a doormat for more assertive managers to get their own way. At some point, you have to stand up.

Sun Tsu, the ancient Chinese philosopher, did not know much about modern management. But he was an expert on warfare. And his first piece of advice is simple: don't fight, unless all three of the following conditions are met:

- There is a prize worth fighting for.
- You know you will win.
- There is no other way of achieving your goal.

Most corporate battles miss at least one of these conditions. Sometimes they miss all three. To misquote another great warfare strategist, Clausewitz, most corporate battles are simply office politics by another means.

So let's see how Sun Tsu can be applied in the office. His three conditions imply you should stand your ground when:

1 **There is a prize worth fighting for.** This means budgets are battlegrounds. Fight hard to get an easy budget at the start of the year, or struggle for the next 12 months to achieve an impossible target: your choice. Other critical, must-win battles are assignments and getting the right team: you do not want to work with the boss from hell or the team from hell. And when you start a new job, negotiate your terms hard before you start: the moment you sign you have lost all your negotiating power.

2 **You know you will win.** This is not just about marshaling all the reason and facts to support your case. Managers use facts like drunks use lamp posts: for

support, not illumination. So you need more than facts: you need political support. Make sure you have a powerful sponsor on your side; make sure you have squared off all the technocrats who can get in the way (finance, accounting, health and safety, HR, etc.) and quietly do a deal to silence potential rivals.

3 **There is no other way of achieving your goal.** There are two problems with fighting. The first is that you might lose. The second is that you might win, and then earn yourself an enemy for life. In the corporate world you need allies and supporters, not enemies who will happily sabotage when the opportunity next arises. The best ways of winning without fighting are:

   a Pre-empt the competition. Get your position accepted before any alternative emerges by lining up support before the formal debate begins.

   b Keep any disagreements in private, so that it is easy for rivals to change their minds without losing face.

   c Publicize any partial agreements loudly: create a bandwagon effect and watch people fall in behind you.

   d Find a win–win: don't just beat the competition. Find some common ground, or some way in which to make them look good. They need to be able to tell a story which makes them look smart, so help them.

Managing across the organization

INTRODUCTION

Look across your organization and see who succeeds and who does not. You can probably find plenty of smart people, some of whom may have MBAs. They have high IQs. You can also find plenty of people with high EQ (Emotional Quotient) who are very good with people and are generally liked. Meanwhile, people who are not so smart and not so nice mysteriously seem to rise to the top. So IQ and EQ are not enough. To succeed, you need something more. You need PQ: Political Quotient. PQ is the art of making things happen through people you do not control; it is about making your limited, formal power stretch so that you have informal power right across the organization. If you can do this, you will set yourself apart from all your colleagues.

PQ is not taught at business school: it is about those hard to define "know-how" skills. And it is also seen as slightly grubby and careerist. This is unfortunate. PQ is the vital skill for the modern organization, where power is diffused, control is ambiguous, and getting things done means doing deals, knowing who to talk to, building trust and alliances, and having a web of influence in the right places. This is the chapter where we start to fill in the holes left by the traditional MBA.

PQ is not taught at business school

NETWORKS OF INFLUENCE

If you want to make anything happen, you need your network of influence across your organization. Increasingly, you will need a network of influence which reaches beyond your organization, as more and more work is outsourced.

The size of your network is not important: collecting business cards is about as useful as collecting beer coasters. Beer coasters tend to be better designed. What counts is:

- **Network quality:** do you know the right people?

- **Network depth:** will people actually return your phone call and react positively to you?

Network quality

As the old saying goes, you are known by the friends you keep. So choose your allies well. This is a harsh truth in many organizations. Winners congregate with winners to form a little magic circle which infuriates everyone else. Put another way, if you want to swim with sharks, be a shark not shark bait. Finding the right network is not a random process of being nice to people with big titles. You need a network that works for you. Your network will be filled with seven sorts of creature:

- **Sponsor.** This should be someone at least two levels above you in the organization who can look out for your interests, see when good and bad opportunities are arising and can clear political blockages for you. In return, sponsors find it useful to have informal eyes and ears telling them what is really going on; they often need a spare pair of hands for some discretionary work and they like having their egos polished by bright young things who appear to value their brilliance, humanity, insight, and all-round business genius.

- **Your boss.** This is the most important person in your network. If you do not like or trust your boss, your boss does not have a problem: you do. You may be taught how to manage a team; learning how to manage your boss is even more important. The essential insight is that whereas your team works on your terms, you have to figure out how to work on your boss's terms without destroying your life and your soul.

- **Technicians.** Corporate life is full of staff functions that we love to hate. These are the people who control us (finance, accounting, HR) and who cannot say "yes" but they can say "no" to any idea we have. Warfare with such groups is tempting but unproductive. Take time to understand the needs of these professionals, respect their need to do their job and work with them, not against them.

- **Your team.** Do not assume that the team you inherit is the team you need. Move fast and hard to put in place the A team. After three months, if your team causes any problems, then they are your problem: you have accepted the team so you have to live with their results.

- **Gatekeepers.** These are the door openers. Some are obvious, such as secretaries and PAs. Treat them like the professionals they are: do not ignore or condescend to them. It is amazing how often they can find a slot in a full schedule if they want to help you. There are some evil gatekeepers: these are executives who tell you that they can help you get a meeting with the CEO or other big shot. In return, they will ask you to make one small adjustment to your plan to make it acceptable to the CEO; then they will ask for another and another and another. They will take control and never give you access. Take care.

- **Influencers.** This is the gossip network which will do two things for you: it will be your early warning system about opportunities and challenges. It can also help you seed ideas and messages with other key players. So you have to work out who has the ear of the big bosses: it might be people in apparently harmless staff functions who are trusted because they are in harmless positions.

- **Allies, colleagues, and competitors.** These are the people who you need to strike deals with on a day-to-day basis to get things done. Remember Lord Palmerston's dictum at the height of the British Empire: "We have no permanent friends or permanent enemies, we only have permanent interests." Understand your allies' interests and you can build a coalition.

Network depth

It really does not matter how many contacts you have on LinkedIn or how many friends you have on Facebook. What counts is whether you have a network that works: will people answer your call and act on your behalf? Or are you struggling to get them to reply to your brilliant and vitally important emails?

The simplest way of gauging and building the strength of your network is to focus on how much people trust you. You can think of trust as having three elements:

- **Values alignment.** Can you show you have similar values to the person you want to influence? This can be personal interests and values. But it has to be professional priorities as well: show that you understand their professional needs and that you can work with them, not against them. At its most basic, respect the other person.

- **Credibility.** Always deliver on what you say, however trivial it may be. Even something as small as sending a promised weblink shows that you do what you say.

- **Risk.** Trust is both analogue and digital. When you are building trust, it is analogue: you build trust slowly as you build credibility. But when you break trust, you find trust becomes digital: once trust is broken, it is very hard to rebuild. So you cannot expect to be trusted on big things immediately: you have to earn the right to be trusted. And once you have won that hard earned right, do not blow it away.

If you have a network of allies who trust and respect you, you have the basic platform for making things happen in the very ambiguous world of the flat organization.

MAKING DECISIONS

For managers, decision making is an art, not a science. It is a deeply political process based on partial and imperfect information. We will ignore minor decisions (do I call on customer A or B first?) and focus on the more substantive decisions (do we invest in the new IT project, enter the new market, change our pricing structure?). In practice, effective managers apply five screens to the big decisions they make:

1 Who wants which option? Business is not a democracy. And if it is, you will find the CEO has 1,000 votes and everyone else has zero votes. Decision making is as much political as it is rational, so work out who wants what. You will not be fired for being part of the consensus, even if the consensus is wrong. Being wrong alone is a very lonely place indeed. Equally, if you have a close decision to make and your team wants option A, not option B, then go with option A: make them take responsibility. It is far better to have a team committed to making a decision they like, than to spend your whole time convincing a reluctant team that your decision is better than the one they wanted.

2 What are the benefits of this project? Benefits normally come in three flavors:

a Financial and quantifiable benefits. This has the virtue of appearing to be rigorous and independent. In practice, most financial benefits cases are only as good as the assumptions which lie behind them, and managers will make the assumptions which suit their case. So the case is rigged one way or the other, and the key test is not "do the numbers look good?" but "are the numbers credible and can I persuade colleagues to support them?"

b Non-financial but quantifiable benefits. These are things like: reduced time to market, fewer defects, less staff turnover. These tend to be weak selling points, until they have been converted into tangible financial benefits: fewer defects means less rework, scrappage, and warranty claims which all have a financial cost.

c Non-financial and non-quantifiable benefits such as "improving staff morale," "enhancing the reputation of the firm." These feel-good benefits have close to zero credibility with the CEO, unless the CEO personally has dreamed up a project with these goals, in which case they become all-important.

With all three flavors of benefit, the question is not "how good do they look to me?" but "how attractive and credible are they to the boss, CEO and other decision makers?"

3 What are the costs and risks of this project? The costs of any project include the three flavors of benefits:

a Financial costs: investment, advertising, infrastructure, sales costs, etc.

b Non-financial but quantifiable costs: time and effort involved, use of scarce resources such as R&D and IT.

c Non-financial and non-quantifiable costs: management distraction, opportunity cost versus not doing other projects.

But the biggest obstacles of all are the perceived risks of the project. The rational risks are relatively simple to deal with. The killers are the irrational risks: will this project make me look good or bad, will it lead to someone else grabbing the limelight, will it cut across another pet project? This is the political underbelly of any decision. For a decision to be successful, you have to align all the constituencies and all their interests before the decision is made.

4 Have I seen this pattern before? Much of management is about recognizing patterns. If you have seen a movie a few times, you know what comes next. If, in management, you have seen the same situation several times, you know what to expect. You can then make the right decision. Old timers will call this "experience" or "business sense." In practice, you do not have to wait 25 years to accumulate the wisdom of experience.

The simplest way is to have a good coach: a good coach is one who does not answer a question with a question. Your coach should be someone who has seen all the management movies many times and can tell you what is likely to happen next, depending on what you choose to do. You can accelerate your experience building by tapping into the knowledge of colleagues. Sales people love showing off their tricks of the trade to other people, and most managers are only too pleased to share their wisdom: it makes them feel valued and important. So use them.

5 How does this fit with the priorities, vision and values of the organization? This is often a very simple way of deciding a close decision. If the firm is serious about customer satisfaction, then you deal generously with the customer's request for a refund. If they pay lip service to customer service, you refer the customer to the customer support desk in Vladivostock. Work out the priorities of the organization: if a decision aligns with the needs of the CEO it is more likely to be approved than a decision which is not aligned.

HOW TO INFLUENCE DECISIONS

I was once head of research for a political party, and it nearly cost me all my friendships. I always had data to back up my opinions and quickly discovered that people prefer opinions to facts. In the world of management, the battle of facts versus beliefs matters. If you understand how bosses and colleagues really make decisions, you are much better able to influence them. Fortunately, the work of Daniel Kahneman (Nobel Prize 2002) on decision-making heuristics shows what really goes on.

people prefer opinions to facts

Simplifying the theory, here is what managers need to know about how colleagues make decisions.

How colleagues make decisions

1 **Anchoring.** Do more or less than 40% of the states in the UN come from Africa? The question is anchored around 40% and most people will guess close to that number. Moral for managers: strike early. Before the budget process starts, set expectations very low, before the planners put in some crazy planning assumption. Anchor the debate on your terms.

2 **Loss aversion.** Losses are not just economic and rational. More importantly for managers, they are emotional: "Will I look stupid if I agree to this?" Reversing a stated position loses face. So keep disagreements private while giving public fanfares even to partial agreements.

3 **Social proof:** if Tim Tebow and Derek Jeter use the kit, maybe I can improve by using the same kit. Some hope. But endorsement works. So get the backing of some power brokers for your idea, and even the flimsiest case can succeed.

4 **Framing.** Do you prefer savings and investment or cuts and spending? Easy choice, except that they are the same thing. Frame the discussion to suit your needs. Language counts, even if you are not an NLP fanatic.

5 **Repetition.** All dictators and advertisers know this. Keep hammering the same message home. Repetition works. Repetition works. Repetition works. Repetition works. . . .

➥

6   **Emotional credibility.** If crime statistics get worse, so what? If my neighbor is
    robbed, crime is getting to be a serious problem. When I get mugged, then crime has
    spiraled out of control into a major epidemic. We believe what we hear and see, not
    what we read. Do not rely on PowerPoint. Make your point personally and personal:
    make it relevant to the person you want to influence.

7   **Restricted choice.** Make it simple for your colleagues. If you offer them 10
    alternatives, they will be paralyzed by indecision. Offer them a restricted choice of two,
    or at most three options: the very expensive option they cannot afford, the very cheap
    option which is no good, and the middle option which you want them to pick.

If you thought decision making was rational, think again. You have to work
the political and emotional aspects of decision making as well. Understanding
decision-making heuristics gives some clues as to how you can influence decisions in your favor.

MANAGING CRISES

Crises are not just inevitable: they are good. They are a great way of separat-
ing out the leaders from the losers. Fortunately, organizational life is the perfect
breeding ground for crises, so you should get plenty of opportunity to display
your talents in managing crises. If you cannot manage a crisis, you cannot
manage the organization, so it is a skill worth building. It is also where you will
achieve far more visibility than in your routine day job, and it will give you a
claim to fame when promotion comes around. So do not run away from crises:
embrace them and make the most of them.

Every crisis unfolds in its own messy way. But here are four basic principles
for turning disaster into triumph:

● **Do not go into denial.** Crises do not solve themselves. If anything, they tend
  to get worse quickly. So recognize the problem and be ready to deal with
  it if it is your crisis. If it is someone else's then stand aside, but be ready to
  respond positively when asked. Do not offer gratuitous help or advice, it will
  nearly always be misinterpreted for the worse.

● **Move to act fast.** Colleagues may go into avoidance or analysis mode
  because that is safe, even if it achieves nothing. This gives you the chance to
  take control, lead, and to make your mark. Even if your first steps are in the

wrong direction, do not worry: most people will be delighted that someone is taking the problem away. You can always alter course as you go along.

- **Over-communicate and build your crisis coalition.** As you lead, others will follow. But part of leading is having a clear and simple story which everyone understands about what you are doing. If you do not provide the storyline, then others will create a story about the crisis anyway: their story will invariably be negative. So keep control of the narrative and make sure all the power brokers support what you are doing and your story. This takes an endless amount of time: crises are time hungry events.

- **Be positive.** Crises are marked by people running round in circles and blaming each other. You will be remembered not just for what you did, but for how you did it. So focus on the right behaviors:

Unhelpful crisis behavior	Helpful crisis behavior
Backward looking	Forward focus
Analyzing what went wrong	Moving to action
Blaming and denying	Take responsibility, be supportive
Breaking half-promises	Delivering on commitments
Fearful, paralyzed through uncertainty	Confident and positive

Crises accelerate your career: you succeed fast or fail fast. Learn to manage them well.

THE ART OF THE GOOD MEETING

Pierre-Francois was *chef du cabinet* of a leading French government ministry. He loved meetings: "They are a great opportunity to sabotage other ministers' plans," he declared, gleefully.

The purpose of meetings is unclear to many managers. Some meetings are held because they are always held. Others meetings are a convenient way of appearing busy while sharing and avoiding personal responsibility for anything. And far too many meetings go on far too long. The Queen has an effective way of keeping meetings short. When the Privy Council of senior ministers meet her, the meeting is a standing meeting. Even windbag politicians get to the point faster when they are forced to stand.

The basic test for any meeting is simple: "What will be different as a result of this meeting?" If nothing will be different, spend the time more productively and have a gossip by the coffee machine. The difference test can be refined into three more questions:

- "What did I learn from the meeting?"
- "What did I contribute or achieve in the meeting?"
- "What will I and others do differently as a result of the meeting?"

A good meeting will have good answers to all three questions for all attendees. If you are invited to a meeting where you expect to draw a blank on all three questions, do not go. If you are inviting people to attend one of your meetings, only invite those who will be able to answer all three questions positively by the end of the meeting. Construct the agenda so that you can achieve this result.

A classic error is to go to a meeting to "get exposure" to senior management. If you do that and have nothing to contribute, then you will have achieved the goal of getting exposure: all the senior managers will now assume you are someone with nothing useful to say or contribute. That is not the best way to establish a reputation. Of course, it may be that the formal agenda offers nothing for you, but the most critical part of the meeting may be the five minutes before and after the formal meeting. This may be your chance to quickly meet someone who has been very hard to reach and to set up a full, follow-up meeting with them.

Life is short and meetings can be long. Do not waste life.

GETTING YOUR WAY IN MEETINGS

When do you push and when do you hold back? How hard do you push? These are mysteries which you'll only learn from experience. But experience is no more than pattern recognition: once you have seen the same sort of movie 10 times, you know what is likely to happen next. So here is what happens in different sorts of meeting movie, and what you can do about it.

- Is the decision important to me? If not, relax. Never pick a pointless battle, and that includes making gratuitous contributions to the debate which may keep one side happy and irritate the other.

- Is the outcome clear? If it is, stay relaxed. Let the debate come to its inevitable conclusion.

- If the outcome is unclear, it is an important decision and you are not in the power seat, do not relax. Be prepared to strike early and to anchor the debate on your terms. Your only hesitation should be to check that none of the big power brokers have a strong view which you were unaware of, or they may simply have information you did not know about. Otherwise, be bold and set the debate. To hedge your position you can frame the debate around three options: two should be easy to knock down and the middle one is the one you want everyone to pick anyway. When faced with objections do not fight them, agree with them ("Yes, that is something which troubled us greatly when we developed the idea, and this is how we dealt with it…").

● If you are in the power seat, you can orchestrate the conversation to get your desired outcome while appearing neutral. Ensure the first person to speak will anchor the debate where you want it to be anchored. Then let the debate roll: everyone will want to be heard. For the most part, everyone is likely to cancel each other out. Once everyone has fought themselves to a standstill, summarize carefully: thank each person for one specific (and of course, brilliant and insightful) comment that they made. They are now 100% committed to agreeing with your summary because it supports them (at least on one point). And your summary will lead you to exactly where you wanted to be at the start of the discussion. End of discussion, game over.

meetings should never be used to make decisions

Finally, remember that meetings should never be used to make decisions: there is a risk that attendees may make the wrong decision. Meetings should be used to confirm in public the agreements you have reached in private. So by the time you get to the meeting, you should know you have enough support, and you should also know who will object and why they will object. There should be no surprises.

SURVIVING CONFERENCES

Corporate conferences cost a fortune and often achieve little. Here is how to make the most of them.

Most corporate conferences have three sorts of session: plenary sessions, break outs and informal sessions. Treat each differently.

● **Plenary sessions** are there to allow the great panjandrum to pontificate. They impress no one except themselves. You will not be missed, so you can drop this session while you do something worthwhile. You can normally pick up a copy of the slides, and colleagues will tell you what it was like. If you see the main speaker, say how greatly impressed you were by the speech.

● **Break out sessions** are where groups of 6–12 of you will be asked for your views. These will be written up on some flip chart and then ignored. Since you will be missed from a small group, attend enthusiastically and make some valid points that support the corporate agenda. Be loyal.

- **Informal sessions.** This is where the true value of the conference lies: at coffee breaks, lunch, and other mingling times. This is your chance to network hard to reach executives and colleagues who have interesting skills and agendas. These informal networking opportunities are not the time to make your full pitch: simply set up a full, follow-up meeting for after the conference. Most people waste this time: they speak to friends and colleagues they see every day back in the office, instead of reaching out and extending their network to other people.

If you are asked to lead a session or provide a booth for the conference, you have a choice. If you have little to say, then say it professionally and loyally with the minimum of effort. If you have something to shout about, then really shout. Invest time and effort in making a splash so that everyone remembers your contribution: this is your chance to make your name. If that means busting the budget to get the booth done very professionally, or if it means getting a speech writer for your speech and an actor to coach you on delivery, then do what it takes. Senior management will remember you not by the countless hours you spent working in the shadows, but by the five minutes you were in the spotlight.

Finally, remember that free booze can be very expensive. There is always someone who does not know the meaning of the word "enough": they make fools of themselves and find that the exit door is opened for them.

CORPORATE ENTERTAINING

There are some industries where everyone seems to have a very low golf handicap and others where you are expected to put your liver on the line. In some industries, corporate entertaining is a mandatory part of corporate life.

Some corporate entertaining is absolutely routine: some managers never eat at home because they have a business breakfast (twice) followed by a business lunch and business dinner. These routine events have an etiquette:

- Avoid talking deals unless your partner wants to talk about them.

- Let people talk about their favorite subject: themselves. They will talk at great length.

- Show interest in your target's stories, find common ground, flatter, and do not compete with their stories.

- Finally, open discussion about the industry as a whole. After gossip about some key players, let the conversation gently migrate to the challenges the industry faces, to the challenges your client faces and what you can do to help. Even now you do not need to do a deal. Simply take the time to understand the target's real interests and needs, then follow up after the meal when you are ready.

Some people never get invited to corporate events; others get invited all the time. That is a problem for you. You may think you have done very well to secure tickets for a play or whatever, but your client may groan at the prospect of being invited yet again to the theater. So if you want to make a mark, you have to be different.

Your goal is to construct an event that gives attendees some bragging rights with friends, family, and colleagues. Then you can be sure that your target contact will attend. You need to do something they have not done before, and which their colleagues have not done before. This leads you to:

- Extraordinary events

- Extraordinary people

- Extraordinary places

The extraordinary events have been largely hijacked by the corporate entertaining industry and are costly. So this leads to extraordinary people and places.

The good news about extraordinary people is that there are lots of them, and most of them are for hire. It might be a top politician, or a very interesting academic or professor, explorer, artist, rock star, or journalist. If you have a conference with a headline speaker, then organize for your target to be at the same dinner/lunch table as the speaker and/or organize a personal introduction. Even the most heavily entertained executive is still star-struck. Offer them the chance of being close to a celebrity and they will suddenly take a great interest in turning up at your corporate event. This does not mean you have to go out and hire Bill Clinton and the Rolling Stones. Look through the pages of speakers' bureaus and you will find a huge array of interesting talent available for a few thousand dollars. Match the speaker to the interests of your client.

Finally, if you do an event then do it somewhere interesting. Some restaurants have private rooms which cost no more than the standard meal. Book it and you are way ahead of people dining in the public area. For larger events, most metropolitan cities have clubs, guilds, societies, and historic buildings that can be booked for an unusual and memorable event.

You do not have to spend a fortune, but you do need to use some creativity to attract the right people. And if you want to attract a number of targets to the same event, be very particular about who you allow to come. If it is an event for CEOs, do not allow them to send their deputy: all your other CEOs will be annoyed.

9

Managing yourself

THE MOBILE MBA

INTRODUCTION

Most of us go through life without fully mastering the art of managing ourselves. And the workplace is not the right place for personal navel gazing. But
work is an important part of our lives, so there are some basic things we need to
figure out to make the most of this slice of our lives.

At its most basic, we have to recognize that we always have choices (even if
some of the choices are very uncomfortable) and that ultimately we are responsible for ourselves and our destiny. We all have our sob stories about how life,
bosses, and colleagues have been unfair to us. That is victim mentality: if I have
ever been a victim, then I have been a victim only of my own folly. Once we
accept that we are responsible for ourselves, then we have taken the first step
toward taking control of our lives and improving our lot. So this chapter is about
how we can make the most of ourselves in the world of work.

ACHIEVING A WORK–LIFE BALANCE

How many times have you heard a work–life balance guru advocating that you
work harder? The work–life balance debate has become a euphemism for finding
ways to work less. This is a surprise because statistically we are the idlest generation in history: we work fewer hours for fewer weeks and fewer years than any
generation before us. But it does not feel that way. And there are some big excep-
tions to the average: some people put in minimum hours, others work endlessly.

To find the work–life balance that works for you, you need to ask
four questions:

1 **Do you want to succeed?** Few people get to the top through idleness.
   Success in any walk of life is hard work. If you are determined to succeed, you
   choose a work–life balance which is more about work than about leisure.

2 **Do you enjoy work?** Whisper it quietly, but work can be good. It gives
   meaning and structure to life. The work itself can be rewarding. If you do
   not enjoy work, then your challenge is not about a work–life balance. Your
   challenge is to find work that you do enjoy. For people who enjoy work, the
   work–life balance discussion is irrelevant.

3 **Do you have non-work commitments which are as important as work
   (such as family)?** This is where the work–life balance debate becomes real:
   you have a real trade-off to make. Flextime, part-time working, and working
   from home can all help at the margins, but they are compromises that
   avoid the fundamental questions about whether you want to succeed and
   whether you enjoy work. The reality is that you cannot have it all: you have to

make choices about what you really want and then make those choices work for you. Wanting perfection and wanting it all is a recipe for discontent.

4 **How much do you really work?** Keep a log for a month. How often are you caught in the rush hour at 7.45am on Sunday morning? How many meetings are you attending at 8pm? Often, the problem is less to do with formal hours and more to do with informal hours. We may leave the office, but the office never leaves us: we have no "off switch." Technology is an electronic ball and chain which ties us in, and the nature of managerial work means that we can always do something more to reach the mirage of perfection. So work never stops in our minds.

The prime solution to the problem of informal work is to compartmentalize your life: use the off switch when you are away from the office. Turn off your mobile, your email and your worry function. See if the sky falls down when you do not answer emails overnight. In some places, using the off switch is seen as a sign of idleness and lack of commitment, in which case you need to ask the first two questions: "Do I want to succeed?" and "Do I enjoy work?"

Perhaps the most important thing to remember is that we always have choices, even if they are uncomfortable choices. Do not simply accept what you currently have: if you like it, make the most of it. If you do not like it, then create some options and make your choice.

MANAGING TIME: EFFECTIVENESS

Time is running out until we reach our inevitable sell-by date. We cannot make more of it and we do not have enough of it. So we need to make the most of it. There are two ways of making the most of time:

- **Use time more efficiently:** fit a quart of activity into each pint of time.
- **Use time more effectively:** focus on doing the right things.

To illustrate the difference, think of Charles Darwin. If you read his *Voyage of the Beagle*, you discover that he was a nineteenth century toff idling his time away as he slowly went around the world courtesy of the Royal Navy. He visited acquaintances, went hunting, and messed around. He would have driven any time efficiency expert crazy. He was so inefficient compared to the school run parent who is simultaneously driving, listening to the radio, having a phone conversation (hands-free of course), giving the kids some quality time, and having the washing done at home in the washing machine. Very efficient use of time. Except, of course, that Darwin will be remembered for slightly longer than the school run parent, because he was being very effective in the use of his time. His idle manner belied an intense curiosity about how species evolved, and led to his revolutionary theory of evolution. What he lacked in efficiency, he made up for in focus.

Ideally, you need to use time both efficiently and effectively. Most time management courses focus on time efficiency. So let's focus on time effectiveness instead. First, try an exercise:

- Remember 10 (or even 20) years ago: what do you remember most about that year?

- How do you want to remember this year in 20 years' time?

Here are some of the things you will not remember this year for:

- Beating or missing budget by 7.23%

- Getting a 3.8% pay raise

- Sending 3,400 emails

- Working 2,125 hours

There are some years where I can remember nothing of note: I succeeded only in getting one year closer to death. That is a lost year. Life should be lived with the record button on and in full Technicolor, so make it memorable both inside and outside work.

life should be lived with the record button on and in full Technicolor

To make the year memorable, set some goals. Some goals may take more than a year to complete. That is good. Set the goal now and work toward it. And to test the value of the goal ask yourself how you will remember this year in 20 years' time. If your goal is forgettable, forget it. Find a more worthwhile challenge.

Once you have set your goal, be ruthless about pruning away everything which does not help you get there. Top chess players, pianists, and performers are notorious for their complete dedication and focus to mastering their craft. As you focus on a goal, you will find that a large part of your daily and managerial life is noise. Cut the noise out and you will create huge amounts of time to focus on the few things that will really make a difference to you.

You have two powerful tools for making sure you focus on the right goals at work:

- Negotiate the right goals at the start of the year.

- Delegate everything you can.

If you cannot delegate well and you work toward worthless goals, no amount of time management training will help you.

MANAGING TIME: EFFICIENCY

Try this exercise. Get a large jar. Put some decent sized stones in it, until the jar is full. Full? There is still plenty of space to put some small stones in until the jar is really full. Full? There is still plenty of space between the small stones. Fill the gaps by pouring some sand into the jar until it is full. Full? Not yet. You can still pour some water into the jar until it really is full.

The jar is your working day. You can get a larger jar (work longer) but ideally you get all your tasks done inside the normal day. The stones, sand, and water are your tasks.

- First, focus on the big tasks. These may take months to complete. Some tasks are so big that they are like stones which will not fit into your jar. So break them down into small, bite-sized chunks. If all you can do today is to have a conversation with one key executive about that task, then make sure you have that conversation.

- Second, focus on the middling tasks, the pebbles in the jar. Find some solid chunks of time in the day when you can make real progress on these tasks and then move on.

- Finally, deal with the noise of day-to-day management (the sand and water). Fortunately, lines and commutes were invented especially for this: deal with emails, routine phone calls, and administration in all the small, dead gaps that you have in any working day. Put dead time to good use.

Beyond this, there are some standard and very useful techniques of time management.

Time management techniques

- **Get it right first time.** Rework is costly: you have to undo what you did, explain it all over again to everyone and restart.

- **Deal with each piece of paper, each email, each phone call once.** Your choices are the five Ds:
    - Decide it (and give your reply).
    - Ditch it, drop it.
    - Do it and do it now.
    - Delegate it.
    - Don't defer it: it will just fester and get worse.

- **Schedule assertively.** Fix meetings to suit your timetable, not others. If you work to others' timetables, your calendar will be a mess and you will have endless dead time.

- **Have a to-do list for today and for this week.** Clear the urgent stuff first so that you can create space to deal with the important stuff. Break the big tasks down into a sequence of small tasks which you can manage.

- **Be flexible.** Ignore the gurus who tell you to rigidly schedule your day, including a spare hour of thinking time. The reality of the management day is a rapid fire sequence of apparently unrelated events: you have to deal with that noise but have enough clarity of purpose to make progress on things that matter to you.

- **Find help.** Don't try to do it all yourself.

MANAGING STRESS

Think back to when you have performed at your best. Was it when

- There was no pressure, everything was laid back, and you were living in easy street?

- When the pressure was on to achieve some challenging goals which stretched your ability and stamina to the limit?

Most people perform best under pressure. So we should not run from the tougher challenges: we should embrace them. They help us learn and grow. They build resilience and may give us a claim to fame when we succeed. Pressure, within limits, is good.

the difference between pressure and stress is control

Even if pressure is good, stress is not good. So what is the difference? The difference between pressure and stress is control. When we are in control we may feel under pressure, but we will not feel too much stress. But when we lose control, suddenly we feel stressed (even if we are not under pressure at the time). This guides us toward managing stress: find a way of getting in control. Here is how we can gain control and manage stress when times are tough:

- **Recognize the problem and deal with it early.** The longer you leave it, the worse it gets. Denial is often a good coping mechanism for dealing with past setbacks. It is not a good mechanism for dealing with current reality.

- **Find something you can control.** By definition, you cannot do anything about things outside your control other than worry. And worry gets you nowhere. So find what you can do and focus on that: it may be something small and simple like seeking advice from a friend, or finding out more about what is really going on. You may only have a small rock to hang on to, but find it. A small step is better than no step.

- **Get support.** This can be emotional support from friends and family but can also be advice and support from colleagues in finding a way forward. A problem shared is a problem halved.

- **Work on plan B.** This means even if plan B requires testing the job market and seeing if there are other opportunities inside or beyond your current organization. As long as you only have a plan A, you are both vulnerable and dependent on outside events and other people. As soon as you have a plan B, you have options, you have more power, and more control.

If you are consistently over-stressed in your work life, then you probably have the wrong boss, wrong role, or wrong company. Or possibly all three are wrong. At which point you need to take control and take responsibility for your destiny: go elsewhere or learn to live with what you have. We always have choices, even if the choices are uncomfortable.

HOW TO GET UP IN THE MORNING

Here are three ways of getting up in the morning. I have tried all three. Take your pick.

- **Option 1.** Wake in the middle of wars, natural and man-made disasters; lying politicians, greedy business people, doom mongering lobbyists and scientists, and scandals and corruption. That is called waking up to the news. Even the weather forecast may or may not cheer you up. Leave just enough time to get to work, so that each traffic delay, red light, or problem with public transport will send your anxiety and frustration soaring. I have tried this option for years: unlike wine, it does not improve with age.

- **Option 2.** Wake up with no radio, electricity, or running water. Your nearest water is 5 miles away in a muddy and crocodile infested river. By the time you have carried the water back, on your head, the temperature will be past 100° and your working day has yet to start. I spent seven years hanging out with tribes like this one in Africa, and started to develop a nostalgia for waking to news of war and cataclysm on the radio.

- **Option 3.** Wake up to your favorite music station. Go to the bathroom and discover a miracle: turn on the tap and fresh, cold, clean water comes out. Just like that. Turn on another tap and find another miracle: hot water comes out, without the need to collect firewood from the bush. After two miracles in two minutes it is pretty hard to have a bad day. Leave for work early, listen to an audio book or music. Feel fresh and relaxed, even if public transport has gone missing.

We can all choose how we feel. If we want to feel miserable, cynical, and stressed then that is our choice: option one will justify our decision. We have now become so used to the luxuries of modern life that we take them for granted. If any of the wonders of modern life go wrong, from traffic to plumbing, we get frustrated. But when we can stand back and admire the miracles of modern living, the world looks pretty amazing.

we can all choose how we feel

Each of us has our own routine and formula for starting the day, and we will all make our own choices about how we want to feel. Choose well.

DEALING WITH ADVERSITY

Bad stuff happens in every life and every career. It will happen, but you do not know when or why or what exactly it will be. Deal with it poorly and it is terminal to your career. Deal with it well and you become more resilient and a better manager as a result.

Your employer may appear to care, but most do not. You can take time off, but all your colleagues and bosses will see you as damaged goods when you eventually come back (unless it was for a few days which you take as part of your PTO anyway). It can be very lonely and very disheartening when the bad stuff happens to you. So how can you cope? There is no easy way out. But here are 10 things that will help.

Ten ways of coping with the bad stuff

1   **Recognize the problem for what it is.** You may well go into a personal valley of death: denial followed by anger and then resignation and giving up. This is natural and human. There is a road out of the valley of death. Others have been where you are and others have found a way out. Work through the inevitably emotional early stages and find the road out of your troubles.

2   **Take control.** Work out what choices you have, however awkward they may be. Identify a few things you can do, even small things, so that you can start to make progress. Move from being a victim of an uncaring world to having some mastery over your own destiny. This is the road out of the valley of death.

3   **Wear the mask.** Leaders learn to wear the mask of leadership: stay positive and action focused. This can be very hard if you are feeling bitter, unhappy, and disappointed inside. But projecting bitterness and anger only makes things worse.

4   **Find some support, ideally outside the organization.** If you confide in your most trusted colleague, you confide in the whole firm. Public confessions are not good. If family and work do not mix, hire a good coach who will provide an emotional outlet and will help you look at your situation more impartially and productively than perhaps you can.

5   **Don't rush.** Act in haste and you may well live to regret it. Email is especially dangerous: one bad email will turn a crisis into a drama.

6   **Always have a plan B.** If your only plan is to work with one boss in one firm in one role, you become a slave. If you have options, inside and beyond your firm, you have more power and more control. And as you work out your road map for recovery, think about your plan B road map. Plan B gives you freedom and flexibility.

7   **Take responsibility.** This is a hard lesson. No matter how outrageously fortune or colleagues have treated you, the only person who is responsible for your fate is you. Somehow, you managed to put yourself in a position where bad stuff could happen to you: you are the solution to your problem. We are also ultimately responsible for how we feel. We can choose to feel miserable; we can choose to feel happy. Our feelings are our choice: do not let others impose feelings on you.

8   **Remember who you are.** The more your identity is based on your work, the more vulnerable you are. But you are far more than an employee: you have your strengths. Build on those.

9   **You are not alone, even though you may be lonely.** You are not the only person to go through hard times. Others find a way through. And if they can survive, so can you.

10 **Count your blessings.** Others have lives that are far harder than anything we care to imagine in the relative luxury of the corporate world. Focus on the good things in your life and remember that happiness is the ultimate revenge. If you are happy, then all the miserable Machiavellian misers who spread mischief will always be miserable and you can always be happy.

WHEN TO MOVE ON

If the headhunters promise you greener pastures elsewhere, remind them that it is greenest where it rains most. Other firms may look better from the outside, but behind the impressive glass and steel facade and the fancy PR, most firms are the same: internal politics and competition, inefficiency, occasional chaos, and intense pressure.

You will never find out the truth about the new organization until you start work there, which is too late. They will always put their best face on to attract talent, once inside you will discover their normal face.

Here are three good reasons for *not* moving:

1 **You do not get along with your boss.** People do not leave their firm; they leave their boss. This is often a mistake. The corporate carousel keeps on turning and your nightmare boss will not be around forever. Equally, the dream boss you think you saw in the other firm will move when that firm's corporate carousel turns again.

2 **You will get more money at the next place.** There are three problems with this.

   a There is no point in earning more money if you end up hating your life.

   b If you are overpaid, you will find you become a slave to the new firm: your family will adjust to the champagne lifestyle, and you will not be able to return to beer wages.

   c Ask yourself where you can increase your earnings tenfold in 10 years, rather than focus on 20% or 30% today, which will seem trivial if you succeed with the bigger ambition

3 You will lose all your networks and power when you move. Your informal power is what makes you effective in your current role: you have track record, credibility, and you know who to call when you need to make things happen. And they will answer your call positively. In your new firm, you have none of these advantages.

Here are three good reasons for moving:

● **You are about to be fired from your current role:** you are far more attractive as a job candidate if you are still employed than if you are a hungry jobless person on the street.

● **You hate your job:** you get up in the morning and your heart sinks at the prospect of the day. You may be in the wrong career, not just the wrong firm.

- **You have genuinely hit a career dead end:** you cannot see sensible progression within your current role and you need to find new opportunities.

If you decide to move, be aware that there are several one-way leaps which you cannot reverse when you have taken them:

- **Stepping off the gold standard.** There are a few gold standard firms that define excellence in their industries: McKinsey in consulting, Goldman Sachs in investment banking and P&G in marketing, for instance. Once you leave these gold standard firms, you cannot get back to that level. So make sure you cash in at the right time for a truly exceptional opportunity.

- **Becoming an entrepreneur.** Once you have tasted the joys and perils of freedom, you will never be able to go back to being an employee. Working for a wage slave who you do not respect becomes impossible. If your first enterprise fails, you will simply have to pick yourself up and start another business, until you finally make something work.

- **Becoming the CEO.** As with entrepreneurs, there is no going back to reporting to other people again. But at least if you fail, your pockets will be stuffed with gold as your reward for failure and you can float off into charity and commission land.

An MBA should teach you to think strategically about your business. Use the same mindset to think strategically about your career.

10

The daily skills
of management

INTRODUCTION

The daily skills of management appear to be trivial: speaking, listening, writing, reading. Learning about them is beneath the dignity of any self-respecting manager, let alone an MBA course. But you can be sure that CEOs are not made or broken by their knowledge of the more sophisticated management tools like Bayesian theory or the Black Scholes option pricing model. They are made or broken by the basic daily skills of management. Similarly, top soccer players are not the best because they have perfected the overhead kick. They perfect their basic skills and will train on the basics every day, just as all top athletes, musicians, and performers do. Only managers think that the daily skills of management are beneath them.

The problem with the daily skills of management is that we all think we know how to speak, read, write, listen and do all the other things managers have to do all day. At a simplistic level that is true: you are reading this, so you know how to read. But now step back. You may know how to read, write, listen, and speak. But what about your colleagues? How many of your colleagues:

- Fail to read, understand, and act on your very clearly written emails and messages?

- Talk a form of incomprehensible management speak, or are just plain confusing and jumbled in their thought processes and what they say?

- Never bother to listen even when you go to great lengths to explain clearly what you mean?

- Write garbage which is either over-familiar gossip or unintelligible and endless prose?

Look around you and there is plenty of evidence that no one else can read, write, talk, listen, or perform the other basics of management well. That is not because they are dumb. It is because the management world is different from the leisure world. We have to learn new ways of using old skills. That does not mean

focus on the most basic tasks and you will shine

becoming a parody of management: using long words which mean nothing, and pretending to achieve things while doing nothing. So what follows is an unfamiliar take on familiar tasks.

The good news is that so many of your colleagues perform the daily tasks of management so poorly that it makes it easy to stand out by being less incompetent. Forget notions of "in search of excellence" and other guru-speak. All you need is to be less incompetent than your rivals and you will succeed. Focus on the most basic tasks and you will shine.

THE ART OF THE PERSUASIVE CONVERSATION

Good managers need to be great persuaders. Some people have natural charisma, wit, and charm. The rest of us have to learn how to get our way. Fortunately, the persuasive conversation is not like a social conversation which rambles off in unexpected directions. Nor is it like a sales pitch where you try to bamboozle your opposition into submission. It is simply a structured conversation. You do not have a script: you have a structure that tells you where you are and when you can proceed to the next step. Once you have mastered the structure, you will find it easy to herd people into agreement with you.

Below are the seven steps of the structured conversation. Think of each step as a set of traffic lights: do not proceed until you have a green light for that step. The seven steps even have an acronym: PASSION.

PASSION: the seven steps

1 **Preparation and purpose.** Be clear about your goal and the purpose of the meeting. The goal may not be to get full agreement, but simply to agree what the problem is. Sometimes it takes a few seconds to persuade someone. Other times you may need several meetings. Understand what their expectations are; adapt your message to their needs. Make sure you have the logistics of the meeting right: right time, place, people, and materials. Finally, once again make sure you have a plan B in case things turn out unexpectedly.

2 **Alignment and rapport.** Get onto the same wavelength as the other person. If you know them well, this may be no more than a quick check to make sure you have them at a good moment: if they are barking with rage because of their previous meeting, they will not be in a receptive mood for your great idea. If you are less familiar with someone, invest time in getting to know them. They are more likely to respond to someone they trust than they will to a stranger. Build rapport.

3 **Situation review.** Understand the situation as your partner sees it: agree how your idea can fit into their agenda. You should be listening more than talking, and when you talk you will be asking questions. As they talk, work out how to present your idea so that it fits with what they want.

4   **So what's in it for me?** You know what you want, but do you know what they
    want? Maybe all you can offer is an easy life if they agree and hell if they do not. But
    find something that makes it sensible for them to agree. Something sensible may be a
    call to the greater good of the firm and profitability; more powerfully it will be to make
    them look good personally.

5   **Idea, stated simply.** State your idea in the language of the other person, and
    briefly explain how it works. Done well, your explanation will pre-empt all their likely
    objections (see 6).

6   **Overcome objections.** If you have been listening properly in steps 2 and 3, you
    will already know what their objections are. Even better, you will have pre-empted
    their objections. You can do this by recognizing their concern; suggest that you
    had the same concern until you realized whatever the solution may be. Never fight
    objections: you invite retaliation. Treat objections as a chance to work together to find
    an acceptable solution.

7   **Next steps.** Be very clear about what happens next and then check that the other
    person agrees. If they do not agree, go all the way back to step 3. The chances are that
    the ground work was not done properly.

As you follow this structure, remember some simple principles about how to
conduct the conversation:

- Listen more than you talk and act on what you hear.

- Understand the world from the perspective of the other person.

- Act as a partner and a colleague: if you try the sales hustle you invite
  resistance.

- Don't hide behind PowerPoint, which immediately sets up an "us and them"
  situation.

- Follow the structure, using each stage as a set of traffic lights which you need
  to turn green throughout.

- Persuade in private, which allows people to change their mind. As soon as
  the meeting is public (which means there is a third person) it becomes very
  hard for people to change their first, casual, opinion without losing face.

LISTENING

All great leaders, sales people and managers have one secret in common. They have two ears and one mouth. Hopefully you share their secret already. Even more important, they use them in that proportion: they listen twice as much as they speak.

Weak sales people and managers think they have to speak to impress and try to talk over everyone else. Shouting longest and loudest does not work. True power whispers and does not need to raise its voice all the time.

true power whispers

To find out how to listen well, blow off work this afternoon and go down to a local coffee shop. Tell your boss you are doing some vital research into a key management skill. You will normally find a couple of people gossiping: often one person does all the talking and the other does all the listening. Observe how the listener listens. The listener will:

- **Look interested:** by maintaining eye contact and leaning forward into the conversation.

- **Mirror the body language of the speaker:** naturally.

- **Empathize:** "How one earth did you get through that?"

- **Encourage:** "I don't believe it! Really?!" (contradictions like this are a wonderful way to make people talk more.)

- **Paraphrase:** "What? They did that straight after breakfast?!"

Back in the office, use the same disciplines. Even the cup of coffee helps if you want them to talk. The most important skill in the office environment is paraphrasing. When you have been listening, summarize what you have heard and replay it back to the speaker using your own words. Paraphrasing helps because:

- **It forces you to listen:** you cannot paraphrase if you have not heard what was said.

- **It helps you remember:** by saying something, it is naturally committed to memory.

- **It gives the speaker confidence:** that you have both heard and understood what they said. This builds trust. It also means that they shut up: they no longer feel the need to go on repeating themselves to get their message across. So your meeting becomes shorter and more productive. In large meetings, this is a good way to cut short anyone who is being verbose: once they know they have been heard, they can relax and stop trying to make their point.

- **It avoids misunderstandings:** if you summarize incorrectly, you will hear about it very quickly.

Paraphrasing turns you from a passive listener into an active listener. Importantly, listening is not agreeing. It is gathering intelligence and understanding, so that when you decide to speak, you speak from a position of knowledge and power instead of ignorance. Listening makes your speaking far more effective.

THE ART OF PRESENTING

There are few good ways, and many bad ways, to die. Perhaps one of the ugliest ways to die is with a hundred bullet points to the head. PowerPoint offers every manager a compelling reason to retire early and start a vegan farm in the sticks.

When offered the chance to present and inflict PowerPoint hell on fellow executives, managers typically fall into two dangerous camps.

First, there are the zombies who have 300 pages of densely written slides, which they proceed to read out loudly and far slower than the audience can read them. After 20 minutes the audience sees that the presenter is still on slide six of 300 and the collective will to live expires totally. The zombies miss the two basic tenets of writing slides for a presentation:

- It is better to have dumb slides and a smart presenter than to have smart slides and a dumb presenter. In other words keep each slide very simple and then let the presenter explain and bring it to life.

- Any presentation or document is like a diamond: it benefits from good cutting. A presentation is only complete when it is not possible to say any less. Many presenters believe the opposite: they think it is complete only when they can say no more.

The second group are nearly as bad. These are the self-important who fill the air with nothing more than their own self-importance. They can bore on any subject, but most of all they like to be boring about themselves. They normally exhibit zero awareness of the three basic principles of presenting well:

- Energy

- Enthusiasm

- Excitement

If you show energy, enthusiasm, and excitement, there is a risk that other people will feel the same way about your presentation and they may even enjoy it. If you are not energetic, enthusiastic, and excited, do not expect anyone to feel enthusiastic for you. If it sounds difficult to achieve these three Es, try the following exercise:

- Present to your spouse the details of the latest cost allocation system in your company. If you fall asleep before your spouse does, you have failed. It is difficult to show energy, enthusiasm, and excitement about topics that do not interest you.

- Tell some of your peers about the most exciting (legal and decent) thing you have done in the past year. The three Es will come entirely naturally to you.

When called on to present, try to find a subject, or a point of view on a subject, which genuinely interests and excites you. The secret of achieving the three Es often comes down to one more E: expertise. If you really know your material, then you will exude confidence and every question will not be a threat, but a chance to shine.

try to find a subject which genuinely interests and excites you

None of us are likely to be great orators, but by keeping things short and simple and working on energy, excitement, and enthusiasm tempered with a little expertise we may well save our colleagues from a very ugly death.

HOW TO USE POWERPOINT

It is 25 years since PowerPoint first inflicted itself on the world. Whether the world is a better place as a result is open to debate. In the past 25 years we have discovered plenty of ways to use PowerPoint badly. Here are 10 tips for making the most out of it.

Ten tips for making the most out of PowerPoint

1 **Throw it away.** You are much more powerful without the crutch of PowerPoint. Really important things never get discussed over PowerPoint. PowerPoint leads to one-way communication, not to discussion. If you want a presentation aid, use a blank piece of paper. Drawing or writing on a blank piece of paper draws people into your magic show, and encourages interaction rather than passive listening and surreptitious texting.

2 **Minimize the number of slides.** A presentation is not complete when you can say no more. It is complete when you can say no less. Focus on the one big message you want your audience to remember. Eliminate everything else. If you have four points per slide and 25 slides, that is 100 points you will make. The chances of people remembering them all, or the one you think is most important, are close to zero. Focus, focus, focus. And the best way of doing that is to tell a simple story which can be summarized in not more than 12 words. That is the most that you can expect anyone in your time pressed audience to remember. And then keep hammering away at the same basic message.

3 **Minimize the words on each page.** Your audience can read faster than you can speak. The idea is to have a smart presenter and dumb slides: the presenter brings each slide to life. Hell is the smart presentation and dumb presenter: highly detailed slides that the presenter slowly reads out loud, without adding any insight. My best presentation is a series of photographs: zero words.

4 **Present to the audience.** No one wants to listen to a presenter who is looking at the screen and talking to his beautiful presentation, with his back to the audience.

5 **Know the purpose of your presentation.** What do you want to be different at the end of the presentation, and for whom? If there are many people in the room, focus on the one (or maybe two) people who you really need to persuade. Your presentation will become more focused, more dynamic.

6 **Energy, enthusiasm, and excitement.** If you are not enthusiastic about your presentation, no one else will be. I once heard Patrick Moore, the astronomer, give a talk. I hate astronomy and loved the talk, simply because he was so enthusiastic about his topic.

7 **Engage the audience.** Make eye contact; encourage interaction. As you prepare your presentation you should keep on asking yourself one question: "Why would person X want to listen to this?" If you are not sure why they would want to listen, then either drop the slide, or make it more relevant and engaging.

8 **Cut the fancy graphics, slide transitions, and other funky stuff.** Do not let the technology get in the way of the message. The fancy PowerPoint technology may look cool to you; it will look juvenile to senior executives who will probably conclude that you have too much time on your hands to waste if you spend it all on fancy PowerPoint graphics.

➡

9   **Rehearse.** Then rehearse some more. Then really get serious about rehearsing. The more you rehearse, the more confident you will become; the easier it will be to engage the audience rather than talk to your slides and the better you will appear.

10 **Start well and end well.** I always have my first 30 seconds scripted in my head so that I can start well, however nervous I may feel. Most people then fall into the trap of not knowing how to finish: they just give up with "any questions?" Make sure you have a good finale which makes your main point and leaves on a high: script it as closely as you script the start.

HOW TO WRITE

No writer should ever write about how to write. It is an invitation to ridicule as readers see the writer is breaking all his own rules. So feel free to chuck the rotten tomatoes and custard pies in my direction as I share what I have been taught about writing. As ever, theory is easier than practice.

Fortunately, we do not have to write like Shakespeare. But by following a few simple rules it will make it easier for us to write persuasively. After years of being beaten up by one editor, I figured out he always called me out with five rules. Here they are:

1   **Write for the reader.** Do not write what you want to write. Work out what your reader needs to hear and why they need to hear it. Then craft your message for that reader. You will find you can reduce your document dramatically this way.

2   **Tell a story.** Marshall your facts into a clear and consistent argument. It should have a beginning (this is where we are, the challenge we face) an end (this is where we are going to) and a middle (this is how we are going to get there).

3   **Keep it simple.** Simple means short words and short sentences. Short is easier to understand than long, and is more likely to be read.

4   **Make it active.** The passive tense is boring and pompous; the conditional sounds uncertain and weasel-like. Use positive language, positive tense.

5   **Support assertions with facts.** The easiest way to kill your credibility is with a false fact or number: once the reader sees one mistake they will assume the worst. In the words of Warren Buffett: "There's never just one cockroach in the kitchen."

Shakespeare probably ignored these rules. But he was a genius, he did not have to write business documents, and he did not have my editor beating him up.

HOW TO READ—AND SEEING THE INVISIBLE

We have a problem. You are reading this (although possibly for not much longer), so why on earth should you read about how to read when you can already read? Because there is a huge difference between reading for pleasure and reading for business.

I thought I knew how to read, until I came across Andrew. We were all sitting in the old-fashioned partners' office. We thought we were all pretty bright, except for Andrew. If we shone as brightly as a hundred-watt bulb, he was a solitary, spluttering candle. But much to our annoyance, all the staff reckoned that Andrew was brighter than the rest of us.

One day, I saw Andrew scribbling away. I asked him what he was doing. "I have some associates coming in with a paper to test me," he said. I had always thought that was our chance to test them, not the other way around. "They want to see if I can add any value to their draft. So I am making some notes." He then patiently explained to me how he would pass his associates' reading test. He had three rules:

1 "Make a note of my point of view on the paper. They are all smart, and I do not want to get caught up in their internal logic." That hurt. I was always getting caught up in the internal logic of what I was reading: I would then find it hard to come up with an original insight.

2 "Make a list of all the topics that I expect to see covered. That helps me see the invisible: what they have not covered in their paper." I was starting to see why they thought Andrew was so smart. I never spotted the invisible until too late: after they had left the room.

3 "Outline a few coaching points I can cover, so that they feel they have gotten something out of me." Now I started to see why they not only thought Andrew was smart, but they liked him as well.

reading for business means reading with prejudice and purpose

I had discovered that reading for pleasure and reading for business are completely different. Reading for pleasure means reading with an open mind, and enjoying the journey of discovery. Reading for business means reading with prejudice and purpose. Eventually, I found that just a couple of minutes' preparation before seeing a paper or hearing a presentation would make me a much more critical and effective reader and listener. Some people even started to think I might be smart. Getting to be liked was an entirely different challenge.… .

COMMUNICATING: FINDING THE RIGHT MEDIUM

Should you communicate in person or electronically: by email, phone, video conference? Because we have the technology we like to use it. That is a universal but unsound human instinct, as demonstrated by the existence of nuclear weapons. We should only use technology when it is appropriate.

There is a simple guiding principle for when to use technology for communicating:

● Transactions can use technology, but

● Trust requires face-to face-communication.

The most common mistake is to use technology to communicate when trust is required, for instance:

● Sending an email to make your position clear on a sensitive issue: you then leave an electronic trail which vindicates you if things get worse. But it does nothing to resolve the issue: talking to the other party might solve the problem, rather than covering your backside.

● Setting a video conference with some key partners/suppliers/customers or vendors in another country. Very efficient and it saves money. But it is ineffective, however good the video conferencing technology is. Seeing someone does not build trust. The small side conversations, the chance to catch a meal with the partner, the get-to-know chit-chat are all lost in a formal video conference. If you want to build a relationship, you have to invest in it: buy a plane ticket and visit them.

● Giving some bad news to the boss over the phone: it has the advantage of being quick and you do not have to confront the ogre face to face. But you miss the chance to gauge the reaction properly. And if you meet face to face, the boss cannot put the phone down on you: you will probably stay until you have worked out a way forward.

If your meeting is about using or building trust, meet the person face to face.

COMMUNICATING: PRINCIPLES AND PRACTICE

Miscommunication is at the heart of too many conflicts and crises in the workplace. We all like to think that we communicate well (speaking and listening) and that other people are at fault: they do not say clearly what they mean and they do not listen. Ultimately, we are all part of "they."

Effective communication requires hard work. Here are five basic principles to follow:

COMMUNICATE EARLY Anchor the discussion where you want it to be anchored. If a rival agenda anchors itself before yours, you will find it hard to shift.

COMMUNICATE OFTEN Repetition works. I use the rule of seven: I do not expect people to have heard, understood and to act on what I have said until I have said it seven times, here is why:

- First time: they literally do not hear what was said.

- Second time: they hear what was said but ignore it.

- Third time: they no longer ignore it, but think it is not important.

- Fourth time: they realize it may be important, but are not prepared to act on it.

- Fifth time: they might want to act on it, but do not yet understand what they must do.

- Sixth time: they now understand what to do, but have other things to do.

- Seventh time: OK, I surrender, I will do it. Now.

BE CONSISTENT Say the same message time and time again. If your message deviates slightly, once, rest assured that everyone will pick up on that and start the game of "I thought you meant…." Assume that anything you say will be misinterpreted. People hear what they want to hear, not what you want them to hear.

KEEP IT SIMPLE You know what you mean and it is obvious to you. Unfortunately (or perhaps fortunately) your colleagues are not psychic and cannot read your mind. And they have other things to think about. Anything you say will not just be misinterpreted: it will be misunderstood. Assume you are explaining your idea to a classroom of primary school children, and then simplify your message further.

USE DIFFERENT MEDIA Some people love email, others do face to face, some prefer the phone, some listen more in the morning than the evening (or vice versa). If the message is important, do what it takes to get the message across in a way that ensures it will be heard.

PROFESSIONAL GUARD

Nothing pleases a newspaper editor more than a good scandal, preferably involving a celebrity. Many political careers, carefully nurtured over decades, have been wrecked overnight by a moment of indiscretion. Your indiscretion may not make the front page of the newspapers, but unlike a celebrity scandal, it is unlikely to be a career enhancing move. Too many careers have been wrecked needlessly: the pain and expense of the MBA and all the late nights wasted.

Even minor indiscretions are damaging. When it comes to promotion time, you will be competing against a horde of other people all of whom have single-handedly transformed the universe, if their promotion packages are to be believed. So you need something distinctive, something by which senior management can remember you. If they remember you for that unfortunate episode at the Christmas party, kiss promotion goodbye.

Here are the three basic principles of "professional guard":

1 **Anything you do, say, or write will be seen by the person you least want to see it.** This includes anything from your social life: Facebook is dangerous. When writing an email assume that the one person you do not want to read it is sent a copy. Gradually, you will find that this principle forces you to be positive and action focused in what you do; being negative and political is simply too dangerous, besides being a waste of time.

2 **Public places are dangerous places.** You do not know who is listening to your phone call on the train, or who might read the documents spread out in front of you. I have benefited greatly over the years with suppliers and rivals from their failure to protect confidence.

3 **Negative comments and actions make you look negative.** It is very easy to slip into gossiping and talking about how terrible the boss is, your colleagues are, etc. Occasionally I interview people who tell me how dreadful their previous employer was: I do not want to work with someone so negative, so indiscreet and who is going to talk behind my back like that. Even if you had a massive falling out, focus on the positives.

ETIQUETTE

Business etiquette is not about knowing what to do with the salad fork. It is about treating people in a way that gets the most out of them. For some managers, this means that etiquette is about bullying, shouting, cajoling, threatening, and demeaning. For the rest of us, there is a better way.

Etiquette is not about the big things like motivation and dealing with conflict. It is about the small things, the everyday incidents of office life. For instance, do you really want to work with someone who is always late, puts his feet up on the table, interrupts meetings to take phone calls, starts texting when you start talking, and never says thank you?

all the small courtesies of business life do not cost you much

Little things count. In Japan, I was struck that my hosts would always escort me personally to the front door on the way out, even the CEO if I had been meeting the CEO. They convey the appearance of caring and making you feel wanted. Ultimately, there is a golden rule to business etiquette: "Do unto others as you would have them do to you." Being prompt, saying thank you and all the other small courtesies of business life do not cost you much. Work out how you like to be treated, and then treat others the same way.

DRESS FOR SUCCESS

Who do you trust most:

- The well groomed and well dressed person in a tailored suit?
- The wild eyed person with matted hair who looks like they have slept in their clothes for the past week?

If you chose the person in a suit, you may well have chosen an expenses cheating politician, a convicted financial fraudster, a megalomaniac dictator, or a greedy banker. And the wild eyed person might be the IT geek who has spent all night working miracles to fix your IT system to prevent it collapsing at the start of business in the morning.

We should not judge people by their appearances and we should not judge books by their covers. But we do.

Traditionally it used to be easy to know how to dress. In the army, you wore the uniform and had the braid if you were a chief. In the highlands of Papua New Guinea, the chief is the one with the big feathers. In the army, you can wear your medals and get respect. In the office, if you wear your MBA degree on your chest, you will not get respect. In the office, as in the army, there used to be a uniform. But the conformity of uniform has been replaced by the uncertainty of choice. The IT firm may want to look funky, laid back, and creative to recruits, and buttoned down, risk free, and powerful to clients: what to wear? In advertising agencies, creative types have one set of rules and account executives have another set of rules.

Short of calling in the color consultants who will divine your perfect color and color coordinate your entire wardrobe in a delicate shade of mauve, we need some simple principles to follow. There are just two main principles:

- Conforming
- Conservatism

Conforming means dress for your context. If everyone else at the conference is going to be in jeans and T-shirt, you will look like a stuffy old fart if you cling to your suit. Like Superman, you need to be able to change wardrobe according to circumstances. Unlike Superman, you should not wear your underpants outside your trousers.

If in doubt about the context, err on the side of being conservative. Within your office, notice how people one or two levels above you dress: take your cues from them, not from your peers. The chances are that your bosses invest more in their appearance than your peers. And if you want to be part of the boss club, it pays to dress by club rules.

THE DIRTY DOZEN: THE LANGUAGE OF BUSINESS

Don't worry about the jargon: at least we all recognize it when we hear it. The really nasty language in business consists of normal words with abnormal meanings. Here are 12 which should put you on high alert

1 **Just.** This is used to make a huge request or error seem trivial as in: "Could you just do this (500-page) document by Monday?," a request best made late on a Friday afternoon.

2 **But.** Remember, whatever is said before "but" is baloney, as in "That was a great presentation, but…," or "I would like to help, but…."

3 **From.** Much loved by advertisers, as in "Fly to Rome from $10" excluding $100 of taxes and other "optional" extras for a flight leaving at 4am, going to an airport about 100 miles away from Rome and the ticket has to be booked one year in advance.

4   **Might** (and any other conditional verb). Might is used to achieve two things: first it sets up a negotiating position as in "I might be able to do that if...." Second, it lays the ground work for excusing failure later on: "I would have done it, if only...."

5   **Only.** Closely related to "just": it is an attempt to make a big request or problem seem small. "It was only a small error... we only dropped one nuclear bomb over London."

6   **Important** (and urgent). Used to puff up any presentation: "This important new product/initiative...." Important to whom? And why? Maybe it is important to the speaker, but why is it to me?

7   **Strategic.** Important, with bells on. See strategic human capital division, formerly known as the personnel department. Also used to justify spending which has no financial payback.

8   **Rightsize** (downsize, best shore, offshore, outsource, optimize, redeploy, downshift, reengineer). How many ways are there of avoiding saying straight up: we are going to lay off staff?

9   **Thank you.** Normally "thank you" is good, except when used by automated voices at call centers saying, "Thank you for calling, we value your call... (and we have so much contempt for our customers that we cannot be bothered to answer your call promptly so we will put you on hold until you give up and try to use our impenetrable and useless online help instead)."

10   **Interesting.** Fear this word. When your lawyer uses it, you are doomed. When your doctor uses it, check your will is up to date. The recession is certainly interesting. A slightly less interesting time would be preferable.

11   **Opportunity.** Because the word "problem" has been banned in business speak, all problems have become opportunities. This means many opportunities are problems. There is a limit to how many opportunities I can solve.

12   **Investment.** This normally means wild and uncontrolled spending on something for which there is no business case. Important and strategic investments are the high road to bankruptcy.

11

Manage your career

INTRODUCTION

The main reason for doing an MBA is to enhance your career. But the one thing they do not teach you at business school is how to enhance your career. Every school has a placement office, which can guide you to the nearest bank or consulting firm. But that is hardly career management. So if you are going to make the most of your time and investment in an MBA, you need to know how to manage your career. A few people get it right. Many more are left making their excuses.

Every career is unique, but there are some consistent signposts to failure and success. This chapter shows what those signposts are and where they point.

PATHS TO POWER

Look around your firm and you can probably find lots of smart people with high IQs and plenty of nice people with high EQs (emotional quotients). Many of them may exist harmlessly in the side waters of the firm, while people who are not so smart and not so nice mysteriously rise to the top of the firm. So something is missing: high IQ and EQ are not enough to succeed. That "something missing" is called PQ: political quotient. As we've seen, PQ is the art of making things happen through other people who you do not control. PQ is vital not just as a career skill, but also as a management skill. PQ gives you the informal power to complement your formal power or authority. Standard operating procedure in most firms is that your responsibility will greatly exceed your authority; your political skills help you bridge the authority gap.

PQ is vital not just as a career skill, but also as a management skill

In career terms, PQ is about finding the route to power. Here are 10 principles to follow.

The 10 principles of PQ

1 **Find the right role in the right firm.** It helps to be the right nationality. There are some foreign nationals running French, Japanese, and American firms. But the overwhelming majority of CEOs and top executives come from the home country of such multinational firms. And within each firm, there is usually a function that is the breeding ground of future talent. In P&G you can have a great career in finance, but the CEO is always a marketing person.

2 **Have a sponsor**, who should be at least two levels above you and should keep on rising in the firm. Make yourself useful; provide information, volunteer some of your discretionary time, flatter the senior executive by asking their advice and treating them as your mentor. Your sponsor will not just coach you, but will guide you in the direction of good opportunities, help you spot landmines before you tread on them, and give you political air cover when you need it.

3 **Build your network.** Remember, you do not need to be liked, but you must be trusted. The more people trust you, the more they will be happy to work with you. With trust, you can strike deals more easily and resolve tensions before full scale war breaks out.

4 **Build your claim to fame, and stake your claim.** All of your peers are as smart and as hard working as you are, more or less. You need a stand-out achievement: perhaps you ran a small unit at an early age and turned it around, or you take on a project with very high visibility, or you take on an expatriate role. All of these are career accelerating moves: you succeed fast or fail fast. So be sure to set the opportunity up for success. And once you have succeeded, stake your claim: make sure that everyone knows that you led a great team to a great success.

5 **Push your interests.** Your interests are not about improving this year's bonus by 10%. Your interests are about increasing your salary tenfold in 10 years. That means you have to get the right assignment, right boss, right team, and right resources. These are the long-term indicators of success. Do not rely on the vagaries of the HR system and hope you get lucky with the assignment process. Luck is not a method and hope is not a strategy.

6 **Manage your profile.** People will remember you as much for how you are as for what you do. So it pays to be relentlessly positive, and focused on action and outcomes. Leave the doubts, analysis, and process focus to others.

7 **Over-invest in opportunities** to gain exposure to senior management. If you have a 10 minute slot to present to top management, make it a knockout 10 minutes. Hire a speech writer on your own budget, get any supporting material done professionally, get advice on what the top managers expect, want to hear and what they do not like. If it takes two weeks of late nights to prepare the 10 minutes, so be it. You will not be remembered for all the late nights you spent on your regular job: you will be remembered by the time you spend face to face with the top managers.

8   **Flatter everyone.** Research shows that there is no point at which increasing flattery becomes counter-productive. People love to hear that they are great people doing a great job. They will love you for recognizing their innate genius, humanity, and hard work which has been sadly neglected in a cruel world by uncaring colleagues.

9   **Be loyal.** Disloylaty is the ultimate sin in any firm. Bosses keep incompetent people far longer than they keep disloyal people, because at least they can trust the incompetent people and know what to expect from them.

10   **Always deliver**, and that means hard work, long hours, and personal sacrifice (unless daddy owns the firm). If you can't deliver you will be like a Rolls-Royce without any fuel. You will look impressive but you won't be going anywhere.

Power and sausages are alike: the end product may be highly attractive, but the process of getting there is not for the squeamish. You decide if you are prepared to do what it takes to get there.

BUILDING YOUR CAREER SKILLS

The skills you need to succeed at the start of your career are not the same as the skills you need to succeed later on. This simple fact causes many people to hit a career brick wall. They learn a set of skills that work well early in their careers: reasonably, they think that doing more of the same will lead to more success. It does not. It leads to failure.

The basic career trajectory is simple: you start by building strong technical skills, you finish by needing strong people, political, and strategic skills.

● At the start of your career you learn a craft skill: accounting, web design, law, teaching, as appropriate. And if you are good at that, you may get promoted. And that is where things go wrong. You run the risk of becoming the "leader in the locker room." You become like the football player that is promoted to manager: you still want to play, but in reality your job is no longer about playing. It is about helping other people play well: selecting them, training them, directing them, and making them work together well. That is what a manager, not a player, has to do.

● In the middle of your career, people management becomes essential. And in the middle you find yourself surrounded by other managers you do not control. And the other managers are the real competition for you: they are competing for the same pot of budget, promotions, and bonuses. And yet you are meant to work with them as a team. So the skills of influence and politics become very important.

● By the top level, strategic thinking becomes important. You have to know how to set a vision and communicate it; how to mobilize and direct limited resources and how to bind your teams together. And, of course, you still need all the people and political skills you learned in the middle of your career.

The good news is that technical skills can be readily learned. There is a body of knowledge that can be transferred from one generation to the next. Technical skills are "know-what" skills and there tends to be a clear right and wrong way of doing things. People and political skills are less clear-cut: you can be right or wrong in an infinite variety of ways. What works in one situation can fail in another. And yet you have to know how to learn these skills if you are to succeed.

HOW TO ACQUIRE THE SKILLS OF THE LEADER

Try this exercise, which I have tried with thousands of executives: "How have you learned how to succeed?" In particular, focus on the skills required of a successful leader, which are people and political skills, not technical skills.

To make the choice simpler, pick two out of the following six possible ways of learning to lead and succeed:

● Books

● Courses

● Bosses (good and bad experiences)

● Role models (inside and outside work)

● Peers

● Experience

Typically, less than 1% of people pick books or courses, which could be bad news for someone who writes books and leads courses. Most people choose bosses, role models, peers, and experience. In other words they choose personal experience or observed experience of people around them.

practice beats theory every time

This makes perfect sense: if you see someone do something well, try to copy it. If you see someone blow up, make a mental note not to step on the same landmine. Practice beats theory every time.

The problem is that experience alone leads your career into a random walk. If you get good experiences, bosses, and roles models, you succeed. Get poor experiences, and you head to a career dead end. So you need some way of controlling your random walk and putting some structure into your experiences.

Books and courses can help you by putting structure into your experiences: you can judge whether your experiences are useful or dangerous and what best practice might look like. They give you an alternative perspective and a sanity check when the world seems to be going mad around you.

But most important is to take control of your career by making sure you get the right experiences: that means getting the right bosses and right assignments. If you do not do this, then you are simply hoping to get lucky with your career: that is not a good way to run a career. You must take control.

HOW TO GET THE RIGHT BOSS AND THE RIGHT ASSIGNMENT

In any organization there are death star bosses and death star assignments. They represent career suicide. Your challenge is to avoid the death stars and attach yourself to the rising stars who can pull you up through the organization. You have to work the system. Here's how:

- **Make yourself busy and indispensable in your current role.** This makes it very hard for anyone to poach you out of your current role against your will.

- **Find a powerful sponsor:** these are the people at least two levels above you who know what is coming down the pipeline and will be able to guide you toward the right role. Often senior executives like to have people they can sponsor. Partly it is an ego trip for them: they like to have someone who seems to respect their advice and admire them. But it is also practical: these people like to have moles in the organization who can tell them what is really going on, and perhaps help out on some non-budgeted activity of theirs, such as gathering information or writing a speech. Make yourself useful to them and they will, normally, be keen to reciprocate.

- **If you see an interesting opportunity arising, hustle.** The easiest way to hustle is to volunteer your services: help out the good boss on the emerging assignment. Show interest and enthusiasm. Most bosses will get the hint fast: they are always on the lookout for good talent. It is best to let them try to poach you: then you will not be seen to be disloyal to your current boss, and you give yourself a strong hand in negotiating the right role. If the boss is a bit slow, then ask if there are any opportunities, but keep your current boss happy as well.

- **Work your network.** Gossip is good. You need to find out what opportunities are coming up before they are put in the hands of HR for staffing. Once the formal processes have taken over, you are at the mercy of a bureaucratic procedure. You may as well spin the roulette wheel. If you hear about the opportunity early, you can take control. Either you put on Harry Potter's cloak of invisibility by working harder and becoming more indispensable in your current role, or you start working your sponsor, calling in favors, and perhaps making yourself useful to the new boss.

MANAGE YOUR BOSS

Much has been said about how bosses should manage their teams. But there is more or less complete silence on a far more important topic for most people: how they should manage their bosses. If we mess up our team, our team suffers. If we mess up our boss, we suffer. And if we can manage our boss, we can manage more or less anyone.

I discovered the importance of managing upward when I picked an argument with my first boss. I was right, and then I was fired. It was a good outcome for all concerned. Learning from experience can be painful. Instead, it is easier to ask bosses what they expect of team members. The answers from 2,000 bosses I have interviewed and surveyed are surprisingly simple. Here are five things bosses consistently expect from their staff:

- **Hard work.** Sorry, there are no shortcuts. One-minute managing may be possible, but one-minute working is not. In the real world, real results take real effort.

- **Be proactive.** Bosses want teams which take the initiative and make things happen. This is good news for people who do not want to be slaves to their boss, but want to have some freedom to think and act for themselves.

- **Intelligence.** This is not about emulating Einstein. It is about being smart enough to deal with day-to-day challenges without always asking the boss, "What do I do next?"

- **Reliability.** Always deliver: if you make a promise, keep it. Bosses hate surprises, because they are rarely good. And they hate the uncertainty of not knowing whether something is going to happen or not.

- **Ambition.** The good news is that bosses encourage ambition. Ambitious people are more likely to make things happen than people with low ambitions, aspirations, and achievement.

These may seem like very low expectations, and they are. The reason that bosses picked these criteria is because they so often see people failing to leap these very low hurdles. If you can beat these hurdles, you will probably beat your colleagues.

most (but not all) bosses are pretty forgiving of mistakes

The good news is that bosses know, from their own experience, that screw-ups happen. Most (but not all) bosses are pretty forgiving of mistakes. But there are some things that they find hard to forgive. The one sin that does not get forgiven is disloyalty. Disloyalty is not just about plotting the overthrow of your boss. It can be failing to stand up for the boss in public when the heat is on; keeping information back; or telling other people first about important developments. The problem with disloyalty is that it breaks the bond of trust between you and your boss. If your boss can no longer trust you, then you will find that there will be a parting of ways. And the parting may not be on your terms.

HOW TO GET PROMOTED

I was chairing the promotions commission. We faced 50 massive documents, which were all unstinting eulogies of various people seeking promotion. The problem was that we only had 25 promotions to give out, and it was impossible to tell which eulogy was the best. In the end, we ended up asking three questions:

1   **Who is sponsoring each individual?** We might not know each staff member well, but we knew all the senior managers who were their sponsors. Some sponsors were credible, others were not. It was easier to believe the promotion packages which came from strong and credible sponsors, than from some weaker sponsors.

2   **What is this person's claim to fame?** Everyone got checks in all the boxes, so that was not enough. We needed something which made them stand out. Successful candidates had done more than overperform against target: they had done a special project, reached beyond their own department, or taken the initiative in some eye-catching way.

3   **What experience did we have of them directly?** Some candidates were invisible. Others had made their mark, sometimes simply by being enthusiastic, confident, and positive.

Clearly, this is an imperfect way of deciding people's futures. And that is the whole point. Corporate life is rarely fair or rational, even though we try to be fair and rational. People who relied solely on the formal promotion process and worked to check all the boxes came up short. Successful people showed a little more political savvy. So if you are in a large machine bureaucracy, you will increase your chances of promotion if:

- You find a powerful and supportive sponsor: ideally this person is somewhere above your boss, and will work the system for you if you have done enough to help and impress your sponsor.

- Make sure you have a claim to fame which is visible beyond your part of cubicle land.

- Remember impressions count. Figure out who is on the promotions commission: being enthusiastic may count as a certifiable mental disorder in some organizations, but in most will help you stand out from the crowd.

It would be nice to think that smaller organizations are less political, if only because the performance of each individual is more visible. If anything, the politics are more intense and more personal because everyone knows everyone else, and because the promotion criteria are often less clear.

HOW NOT TO GET PROMOTED

Leading from the middle is the hardest stage of any manager's career. Whisper it quietly, but top management is far easier and more rewarding than middle management. At the top you have more control over your destiny, and more resources at your disposal.

Many people never make it out of the matrix in the middle of most organizations. Here are the five most common types of career hold-up:

1 **The boy scout or girl guide**, who believes that working hard and honestly will get you to the top. No it will not. You need a claim to fame, to stake your claim, and to have sponsors who will look out for you at promotion, bonus, and assignment time.

2 **The expert**, who gets promoted on the basis of deep functional expertise. These people are good at managing ideas and techniques: think accountants, lawyers, IT specialists. They fail to learn the top management skills of managing people, politics, and business.

3 **The politician**, who is the opposite of the boy scout. Politicians always "associate themselves with success." They vanish when there is trouble. They plot and connive. They can go far, but most get caught in the end: their enemies multiply over the years and eventually people notice that the politicians have not actually achieved anything.

4 **The autocrat**, who acts like they already are top managers. Their version of being a team player is "play my way or you are not a team player." Again, they can go far, but they are often highly divisive. Like the politician, they acquire enemies who are only too happy to stick the knife in as soon as the autocrat has an inevitable set back.

5 **The cave dweller.** Most large organizations have functional silos and layers like a pancake. When you cross a silo with a pancake you get a cave: this is where some middle managers hide. They protect their little piece of territory, to recreate the certainty they enjoyed in junior management. They fail to work with the complexity, ambiguity, and opportunity which large organizations offer.

So how do you get through the middle management minefield? Successful middle managers all have elements, but not to excess, of the boy scout (hard work) and the politician (understand the organization) and the autocrat (make things happen). Most, but not all, are very good at working with people.

Inevitably, the skills that leaders really need to learn are ones for which there is precious little training. You have to discover the skills and the rules of the game yourself: many middle managers stay in the middle because they never discover the rules of the game for getting to the top.

HOW TO GET FIRED

Most bosses are reasonably forgiving. They will forgive bad hair, bad dress, and bad jokes. Within reason, they will even forgive poor performance and poor behavior. There is one sin which bosses never forgive and *traitors never survive* for which there is no second chance: disloyalty. As soon as you are seen to be disloyal, the bond of trust between you and the boss is broken. It may be weeks or months before you find yourself being eased out or moved on, but traitors never survive.

Think about your own situation: do you want to work with a team you do not trust?

Disloyalty is not just about plotting to displace the boss. Disloyalty is often much simpler, for example:

- Gossiping negatively about the boss around the water cooler: such gossip travels fast and in the wrong direction

- Failing to follow the company line or policy

- Trying to shift the blame for a problem onto the boss

- Failing to speak up in support of the boss when the boss is in a tight situation

- Hiding bad news from the boss, who only finds out about it by accident (in a meeting with the CEO, for instance): maximum embarrassment and the boss looks out of control

You do not have to be a "yes-man." Stand up to your boss and argue, in private so that you do not cause loss of face in public.

TEN STEPS TO A GOOD CV

I have had the doubtful pleasure of sifting through several thousand CVs, looking for the people we need to interview. You need your CV to stand out. You are only as good as you appear on your CV.

Ten rules for a good CV

1   **Follow the format.** If the employer wants your information in a certain way, provide it that way. If you cannot be bothered to format your experience, the employer will not be bothered to interview you.

2   **Avoid mistakes** of substance, style, fact, grammar, spelling, and layout. A sloppy CV makes for a very easy decision: goodbye. Check, check, and check again before submitting your CV. Ideally, get a friend or trusted colleague to check it as well.

3   **Focus on your achievements, not on your responsibilities.** Even the toilet cleaners have fancy titles nowadays. Titles do not impress: what counts is what you have done.

4   **Be positive.** We all have setbacks and failures: they may come out in an interview. The CV is where you present your best face to get the interview. And never be negative about a previous employer: if you are the sort of employee who whines about employers, you will be toxic to all employers.

5   **Demonstrate you have the relevant skills.** Everyone says they are energetic, committed, great team workers, action focused. Instead of saying it, prove it by showing what you have done: "organized a conference for 1,500 people," "doubled unit profitability over three years," "led my sports team to promotion."

6   **Be truthful.** Good interviewers and screeners spot gaps and hype fast. Even if you slip through the net and get a job, a false CV provides grounds for dismissal. Not worth the risk.

7   **Customize your CV.** Highlight the experience and skills that the employer is looking for. Add a short cover letter saying why you are interested in them and why they ought to be interested in you. By implication, this means doing your homework on the employer to understand if you really fit with them.

8   **Avoid unnecessary detail.** Irrelevant information may overwhelm you. Personal interests are a classic disaster zone where I have caught people claiming interests they know nothing about, or having wildly inappropriate interests for the sort of job on offer.

9   **Mind your language.** Passive language is boring. Power language is not credible: it becomes hype. If you make a claim, support it with facts, not hype.

10   **Follow up.** Be prepared to be quizzed in detail on every line of your CV.

WHAT YOUR CV REALLY SAYS ABOUT YOU

Your CV should trumpet your many unique strengths. Experienced CV reviewers know that most strengths also reveal a weakness, so they routinely look at the other side of the precious coin you are presenting to them. What you say and what they hear are quite different things. This is what they find when they look at your CV or at a reference you have provided:

- **Analytical and insightful.** Doesn't get people and achieves nothing.

- **Very goal focused.** Ambitious, tramples over people.

- **Entrepreneurial.** Not a team player; largely uncontrollable; won't fit in.

- **Great team player.** Yes man; little drive or initiative; blindly follows insane orders.

- **Good networker.** Politically devious and untrustworthy.

- **Honest and reliable.** I can find no meaningful strengths in this person.

- **High achiever.** Puts self ahead of anything or anyone else.

- **Empathetic.** Likes hugging people and trees; expect neither action nor insight.

- **Mature.** Past it, low energy levels.

- **Expert.** Anorak who will bore you to tears, cannot manage and lives in a silo.

- **Strong values.** Opinionated, fully signed up member of the awkward squad.

- **Outstanding leader.** "My way or no way" person who does not like working for others.

- **Diligent.** Boring plodder who stays in the box.

- **Action oriented.** Shoots first, thinks second; dangerous liability.

- **Strong track record of success.** Good at telling fairy stories; likes to steal the credit.

All of this confirms what most job seekers fear: you can't win. Whatever you say or do will be taken down as evidence and will be used against you. But at least if you know how your cynical interviewer will twist everything against you, you will be better prepared for the ritual humiliation of the interview process

MANAGE YOUR PROFILE

Mark Othello's words well: "Reputation, reputation, reputation! Oh, I have lost my reputation! I have lost the immortal part of myself, and what remains is bestial." Reputation is everything. And this is where you discover that you have three lives with three different reputations:

- Your self-image and the reputation you think you deserve

- Your reputation as colleagues perceive it (claim to fame and style)

- Your reputation as captured by technology

More or less invariably, our own view of our reputation is better than our other two sorts of reputation. But it is our reputation as seen by colleagues and captured by technology which counts: our self-image is important, but only to ourselves.

WHAT IT TAKES TO BE A LEADER

Most leadership gurus tell you half the truth, at best, about what it takes to be a leader. They will tell you about the need for vision, handling people, dealing with crises and all the other good stuff that makes up the corporate speaking circuit. Here are 10 vital qualities you are less likely to hear them talk about:

The 10 vital qualities

1 **Sleeping on planes and dealing with jet lag.** In any large organization, a leader will spend a large amount of time on planes: I did 250,000 miles a year. The routine was simple: one glass of champagne and one melatonin pill 40 minutes before take-off, and I would be able to sleep all the way. Business class is not for fancy meals and watching movies: it is for work or sleep.

2 **Working in vehicles.** If you cannot work in taxis and cars, you will waste more time than you can afford. Staring out of the window mindlessly is not good.

3 **Dieting.** Leaders are surrounded by biscuits, cookies, and other corporate death food; and then there are the inevitable lunches, dinners, and hotel breakfasts. Either learn to love the fruit, or start jogging. Or die early as an obese alcoholic. But to this day, some firms demand that you "put your liver on the line": if you do not drink and entertain, you fail. Pick your diet to fit your firm.

4 **Ruthless time management.** Lines were invented to let leaders catch up with emails and phone calls; ditch or delegate everything you can; fix appointments around your schedule, not around other people's.

5 **Work the politics.** Find the right assignments, right support, and right mentors. Set expectations well. Negotiate budgets hard. Wake up to the reality of corporate life.

6 **Be ambitious**, for your organization and yourself. Stretch yourself and your team to achieve more than ever; keep on learning and growing. Don't accept excuses, don't be a victim: take responsibility.

7 **Learn to speak well:** to small groups, to individuals, and to large groups. As one tribal elder told me: "Words are like gods: words create whole new worlds in someone's head. So use words well." For many people, having a tooth extracted is less daunting than speaking in public. But it is a skill anyone can develop, with practice, over the years. And leaders must have this skill.

8   **Be able to deal with the tantrums:** be they moody receptionists, clients, or staff, while being positive and constructive all the time.

9   **Learn to be unreasonable in setting goals** and not accepting excuses: know how to stretch people to overachieve.

10 **Have endless self-confidence and resilience**, especially when disaster looms and everyone else is running around like a headless chicken: take responsibility, take control, take action, and move to the solution.

These qualities add up to a person who is pretty driven. Leaders are often not comfortable people to be with. Not surprisingly, many people prefer to keep their humanity and their life than make the sacrifices to get to the top.

When I first started out, my boss told me: "One of the benefits of this job is that you will never suffer the rush hour. You will arrive before it and leave after it." And if you keep that lifestyle going for 10–20 years, you can reach the top. It was not a good choice, but at least it was a clear choice.

Choose well, and whatever your journey, enjoy it.

Index

FINANCIAL TIMES

In an increasingly competitive world, it is quality of thinking that gives an edge—an idea that opens new doors, a technique that solves a problem, or an insight that simply helps make sense of it all.

We work with leading authors in the various arenas of business and finance to bring cutting-edge thinking and best-learning practices to a global market.

It is our goal to create world-class print publications and electronic products that give readers knowledge and understanding that can then be applied, whether studying or at work.

To find out more about our business products, you can visit us at www.ftpress.com.